I0168775

# THE
# KADDISH
# MINYAN

## FROM PAIN TO HEALING:
## TWENTY PERSONAL STORIES

## EDITED WITH AN INTRODUCTION BY
## RABBI HERBERT A. YOSKOWITZ

Second expanded edition of
*The Kaddish Minyan: The Impact on Ten Lives*

EAKIN PRESS ✦ Fort Worth, Texas
www.EakinPress.com

# What Others Said About the First Edition,
## *The Kaddish Minyan: The Impact on Ten Lives*

"There is no time when people need the guidance of religion more than in the shadow of bereavement and loss, and there is nothing that our Jewish tradition does better. This book will help people understand why and how." **—Rabbi Harold Kushner, author of *When Bad Things Happen to Good People***

". . . the most eloquent affirmation I have ever read of the kaddish prayer. For anyone who has experienced the loss of a loved one, for anyone who struggles with the meaning of death and mourning, this book offers wisdom, strength, and healing. This is a gift for the soul. Be certain to read it." **—Rabbi Charles A. Kroloff, president, Central Conference of American Rabbis; senior rabbi, Temple Emanu-el, Westfield, New Jersey**

". . . a touching epitaph to the lives of many people even as it is a living testimonial to the healing process of those who are mourning the loss of a dear one . . ." **—Rabbi Vernon Kurtz, president, Rabbinical Assembly; rabbi, North Suburban Synagogue Beth El, Highland Park, Illinois**

"Skillfully combining eloquent personal testimonies with lucid and learned essays ... Rabbi Yoskowitz has provided a valuable resource for the bereaved who seek solace and support within the Jewish tradition." **—Rabbi Samuel M. Stahl, Temple Beth-El, San Antonio, Texas**

". . . a great gift to all who have and will join the ranks of mourners. Therefore all of us will find this book enlightening and deeply moving . . ." **—Rabbi Samuel Egal Karff, Congregation Beth Israel, Houston, Texas**

"OUR PRAYER BOOKS now vary by denomination but the Kaddish speaks to and for all of us. And so does [this book]...Kaddish means 'to sanctify.' This book sanctifies and adds meaning to the central prayer and the central experience that we all share..." —**Rabbi Mitchell Wohlberg, Beth Tfiloh Congregation, Baltimore, Maryland**

"...A POWERFUL AND POIGNANT SERIES of meditations on the Kaddish prayer, and the experience of mourning. Readers of all faiths will benefit from its deepening insights."—**Rabbi David Wolpe, Sinai Temple, Los Angeles, California; Author, *Making Loss Matter***

"WHAT A BEAUTIFUL, POWERFUL BOOK! *The Kaddish Minyan* has opened this Christian's eyes to the profound spiritual experience of saying Kaddish with others...should be read by Christians as well as Jews..."
—**David Blewett, Executive Director, The Ecumenical Institute for Jewish-Christian Studies, Southfield, Michigan**

"RABBI YOSKOWITZ HAS GATHERED...a rich collection of personal reflections by people for whom bereavement became a path to spiritual renewal. These messages can do the same for many of us as we struggle to make sense out of life just when it seems hardest to do so."—**Rabbi Mark G. Loeb, Beth El Congregation, Baltimore, Maryland**

"RABBI YOSKOWITZ'S BOOK IS A GIFT...While the experience of mourning is universal, and the words of Kaddish are fixed, this book allows us to hear a myriad of distinct voices that inspire us to seek our own reservoirs of comfort from the wellsprings of the Kaddish tradition."
—**Rabbi E. B. Freedman, Director, Jewish Hospice and Chaplaincy Network, Southfield, Michigan**

Copyright © 2003
By Rabbi Herbert A. Yoskowitz
Published By Eakin Press
An Imprint of Wild Horse Media Group
P.O. Box 331779
Fort Worth, Texas 76163
1-817-344-7036
**www.EakinPress.com**
**ALL RIGHTS RESERVED**
1  2  3  4  5  6  7  8  9
ISBN-10: 1-68179-117-3
ISBN-13: 978-1-68179-117-X

The first excerpt on page 78 ("Tradition") is reprinted with permission from the Central Conference of American Rabbis. The excerpt on pages 78-79 ("The Kaddish") is reprinted with permission from The Prayer Book Press of Media Judaica, Inc. The last excerpt on p. 79 ("Personal Meditation") and excerpts on pages xx-xxii are reprinted with permission of The Rabbinical Assembly.

## Dedication

To my family, especially to my wife, Rachel, who faithfully said Kaddish for her mother during the year of mourning. She served as a model for our family on the way to respect a parent when there would be no "thank you" forthcoming.

# Contents

# Personal Page

## Name of Deceased

English Name: _____

Hebrew Name: _____

## Date of Death (*Yahrzeit*)

English Date: _____

Hebrew Date: _____

## Conclusion of Shloshim (first thirty days of mourning)

English Date: _____

Hebrew Date: _____

## Conclusion of eleven months of Kaddish

English Date: _____

Hebrew Date: _____

## Dates of Yizkor

English Dates: _____

Hebrew Dates: _____

# Personal Page

## Name of Deceased

English Name: _____

Hebrew Name: _____

## Date of Death (*Yahrzeit*)

English Date: _____

Hebrew Date: _____

## Conclusion of Shloshim (first thirty days of mourning)

English Date: _____

Hebrew Date: _____

## Conclusion of eleven months of Kaddish

English Date: _____

Hebrew Date: _____

## Dates of Yizkor

English Dates: _____

Hebrew Dates: _____

# Personal Page

## Name of Deceased

English Name: _____

Hebrew Name: _____

## Date of Death (*Yahrzeit*)

English Date: _____

Hebrew Date: _____

## Conclusion of Shloshim (first thirty days of mourning)

English Date: _____

Hebrew Date: _____

## Conclusion of eleven months of Kaddish

English Date: _____

Hebrew Date: _____

## Dates of Yizkor

English Dates: _____

Hebrew Dates: _____

# Personal Page

## Name of Deceased

English Name: _____

Hebrew Name: _____

## Date of Death (*Yahrzeit*)

English Date: _____

Hebrew Date: _____

## Conclusion of Shloshim (first thirty days of mourning)

English Date: _____

Hebrew Date: _____

## Conclusion of eleven months of Kaddish

English Date: _____

Hebrew Date: _____

## Dates of Yizkor

English Dates: _____

Hebrew Dates: _____

# Foreword to *The Kaddish Minyan*

The Jewish spirit heals through community and tradition. It is through these two interacting spheres of text and context, of Torah and fellow travelers, that we reach for strength, support, meaning, and guidance. Sometimes we may achieve profound inspiration or uplifting transcendence—and sometimes we simply manage to make it from Monday to Tuesday, in one reasonably intact piece.

This wonderful publication reflects the encounter of Jews wounded by the death of a dear one with the depth and breadth of remarkable structures: the ancient words of the Kaddish, and the contemporary *Kaddish minyan*. The open, honest voices of these mourners weave an extended family, a "meta-minyan," of empathic, attentive Jews, and simultaneously invite us to recount and listen to our own inner narratives of loss, survival, and growth. Let the information and insight on these pages illumine your own path through grief and inform your efforts to be present with, and supportive of, others in their time of need.

Just as the bereavement extends way beyond the initial shiva week, the shloshim month, and the first year of loss, so the spiritual resources of words and fellowship are ever there for struggle and renewal. *The Kaddish Minyan* models how the memory of a loved one might be restated, rekindled, and revisited; and, as time goes by, how the healing narrative can grow to include anecdotes about that very remembering, about our rebuilding and reaffirming.

This, then, is not only about the journey towards affirming the Sacred in the midst of loss, pain, and despair; it is an echo, a refraction of that very Wholeness and Eternity, much like the Kaddish prayer itself. It is a chorus of searching, soulful Jews, wanting to heal but also willing to help heal others, most of whom they will never know.

Rabbi Simkha Y. Weintraub, CSW
Rabbinic Director,
National Center for Jewish Healing

# Acknowledgments to the First Edition

On a balmy, November 1999 evening at Adat Shalom Synagogue in Farmington Hills, Michigan, I was blessed to be a part of the most memorable adult education program of my thirty-year rabbinic career.

Never before had I experienced emotion such as was expressed during that evening when congregants came forward to discuss what Kaddish means to them. It was a unique moment in time when all of us were at one, enveloped in thoughts of what Kaddish and the *Kaddish minyan* can do for Jews in the throes of dealing with loss. It was this experience and the dialogue afterwards that led to this book.

To all those who were present at the birth of this publication on that evening at Adult Jewish Education, I am indebted.

To my dedicated clergy colleagues at Adat Shalom, whose words and support aided this publication, I am appreciative.

To the congregation's leadership who encouraged and reviewed this manuscript as it evolved—Dr. Michael Gellis, Terran Leemis, Beverly Liss, and Larry Wolfe—I am thankful. I treasure the time we spent discussing this manuscript in my office.

To the loyal readers of this manuscript, including Rabbi Samuel Stahl, David Blewett, Bill Liberson and David

Techner, I am grateful. They critiqued my work and expanded the possibilities of this book to serve both Jews and non-Jews. I am in your debt.

To my secretary, Charlotte Fiszbein, who was very helpful in preparing drafts of this publication, I am indebted.

To Ed Eakin and Virginia Messer, publisher and associate publisher at Eakin Press, and to Melissa Locke Roberts, editor, I express much appreciation.

To Rabbi Simkha Weintraub of The National Center for Jewish Healing, whose dialogues with me about the *Kaddish minyan* increased my enthusiasm to move it towards publication even as his comments made the book's message more poignant, I am relishing the memories of our interesting conversations.

To all those who contributed their reflections on saying Kaddish for a loved one, I am filled with admiration. Their essays are the core content of this book. These wonderful people were willing to share of themselves even in the midst of their grief. They have my deep respect and gratitude.

—HERBERT A. YOSKOWITZ
Farmington Hills, Michigan
June 2001

# Kaddish: An Opportunity to Comfort
## By Rabbi Herbert A. Yoskowitz

Reprinted from the *United Synagogue Review*,
Fall 2002

"Nothing will fill the hole my Dad's absence has left in my world. No prayer has provided me with the guidance or answers that he was so brilliant at giving. But what the Kaddish gave me was sacred time to be a mourner. Not just for seven days of *shivah*; or those first few weeks when people were giving me their condolences. But every day for a year. I stood up in a room, embraced by community, and identified myself as someone in mourning, which was exactly how I felt."

These words—written by a young woman who had just completed a year of mourning—reflect the significant effect of the Kaddish, and of the *Kaddish minyan*, on her life. Indeed, many who have recited the Kaddish for a parent, or for a relative for whom saying Kaddish is required by Jewish law, acknowledge that the Kaddish is a gift to them, not just to the people for whom the prayer is recited.

Most people do not know very much about this prayer or about the structure in which it is to be said. Perhaps they have seen only the example of their parents saying Kaddish and feel compelled to pay the same honor to their parents.

In response to the many questions I received on the Kaddish over the years, I shaped a series of three adult education programs at Adat Shalom Synagogue in Farmington Hills, Michigan. The first and third sessions focused on the history and rational elements of the Kaddish, as well as on its mystical elements. Sandwiched between was a session on individual stories told by members who were in their year of mourning.

Program panelists included a couple who were saying Kaddish for their daughter, a magnificent young woman who lived only seventeen years but who has left an unusually rich legacy. In her "Make A Wish" project, she prepared and appeared in a public service announcement on how young people with cancer like to be treated. This "infomercial" is broadcast nationally. Two other panelists were saying Kaddish for a husband and for a father, respectively. Though only one of the four was obliged to say Kaddish for eleven months, they all decided to say the prayer for that period of time.

In each of the personal reminiscences, there was at least one deep psychological insight. For one panelist, saying Kaddish was "a means of honoring our daughter and gaining comfort, but, most of all, reaffirming my faith in God. It is my faith that has given me strength these past two years. If it were not for my faith in God, I would never have been able to handle this tragedy." When he said the Kaddish, he was at peace. "I feel as if I am a *tallit* and I am wrapping myself around her, giving her comfort. In reality, I know that she is the one that is giving me comfort."

Commenting on the *Kaddish minyan*, another panelist referred to her new "club." "I am a member of a very precious club that I did not choose. My comrades have all been wounded. They acknowledge me with a sweet smile. They understand how fragile life is. They understand my pain as I do theirs. They comfort me as the words of the Kaddish do. I am at peace."

A bereaved widow wrote: "When I recite the Kaddish, I think of my husband. I feel that this is something that I can do for him, for me and for us. Starting my day here gives me purpose."

The fourth panelist reflected on the effect of the approaching completion of saying Kaddish for eleven months for his father: "The Kaddish experience acted not only as a healing exercise but a strengthening bond between myself, my father, my grandfather, and those who preceded them."

In my thirty years as a congregational rabbi, I had never before experienced the emotion generated from that panel, not only from the speakers but from the audience as well. On the day after the presentation, some congregants made contributions to the synagogue in appreciation of this program. Others wrote unsolicited remembrances of their own experience of saying Kaddish for a dear one. Even now, many months later, I continue to receive such remembrances. This emotional outpouring, coupled with my recognition of the need for people to understand the context of the Kaddish prayer, led to the development of *The Kaddish Minyan: The Impact on Ten Lives*, a small volume of personal experiences which I subsequently compiled and edited.

People continually talk to me about their personal journeys during the months of their obligatory period for saying Kaddish. Recently, I received two essays written in different parts of the country, both of which included a theme I had not previously considered. Both writers—one on the West Coast and one in the Midwest—wrote that saying Kaddish in a *minyan* for the full eleven months was the first posthumous gift given to each of them by the parent for whom Kaddish was being recited.

Telling the story of one's journey during and after saying Kaddish for a deceased relative can also benefit one's synagogue, since fellow congregants who read about the experiences will be able to relate emotionally to the "storytellers" as they report on their travels along the road from mourning to wholeness. Our synagogues can apply this model—one member telling another his or her story—to many different aspects of Jewish life, whether life-cycle events or the paths that have brought individuals to live in a better place. Shared stories can heal, whether the subject of the story is adoption, illness, or surviving trauma.

Jason Miller, a rabbinic intern at Congregation Agudath Israel in Caldwell, New Jersey, has used the personal stories in my volume to help people who have experienced the loss of a spouse. Other synagogues have focused on the *Kaddish minyan* as a tool to help congregants heal after experiencing a trauma or a loss of some kind. Rabbi Gerald Zelizer of Neve Shalom in Metuchen, New Jersey, has pointed out the importance of teaching Jews to understand the larger meaning of the Kaddish ritual. According to Rabbi Zelizer, Neve Shalom congregants who read my volume during *shivah* learned more about the meaning of Kaddish and were motivated to recite it "*al pi halakhah*," according to *halakhah*.

The Kaddish prayer and the *Kaddish minyan* have helped many Conservative Jews deal with loss and move toward healing. Programs that highlight the stories of those who say the Kaddish faithfully can help to provide strength, guidance, and nurturing to others in the congregation.

# Preface to the Second Edition

The attestations in the first edition of *The Kaddish Minyan* were read throughout the United States and elicited responses in writing from several readers of the book. Some of those writings are included in this second expanded edition of *The Kaddish Minyan*.

This second enlarged edition, *The Kaddish Minyan: From Pain to Healing: Twenty Personal Stories,* includes unique features which were not present in the first edition.

While the new testimonies included in the second edition come in the main from the Midwest, one comes from as far east as Rhode Island and another as far west as California.

These new testimonies were written by members of daily *minyans* in Conservative, Orthodox, and Reform congregations.

No matter the locale and no matter the wing of Judaism, each contributor during the period of his or her grief aligned with life, with family, and with community. Each found a way—no matter how challenging the circumstance—to attend to the ritual component of the healing process by saying Kaddish in a *minyan*. By telling their stories in this book, they become comforters not only to those mourners who attend services with them but to a wider audience whom they will likely never see.

Each affirmed that only by saying Kaddish in a quorum

for a loved one and not by hiring a surrogate to do so can one derive spiritual strength. Dr. Ismar Schorsch, the Chancellor of The Jewish Theological Seminary of America, pointed out to me what Dr. Solomon Schechter said in a similar context: "We cannot have our love letters written for us. We must write them ourselves, even at the risk of bad grammar." (Solomon Schechter, *Seminary Addresses*, 1959, p. 242)

There is another new component to this second expanded edition. A member of our congregation, Adat Shalom Synagogue, suggested that a disc be made available to help mourners who had trouble reading even the transliteration of the Kaddish. During her week of *Shiva*, his sister-in-law had asked if she could listen to the Mourner's Kaddish and to the Rabbis' Kaddish on a tape or on a disc to help her as she struggled to say each word correctly and to pause at the correct times. He asked me if I could be of help to her.

In response, this volume includes a professionally prepared CD of the Mourner's Kaddish and of the Great Kaddish which became known as the Rabbis' Kaddish or *Kaddish D'Rabbanan*. The latter requires some explanation.

At the completion of the recitation in a quorum of a Scriptural or Talmudic text, everyone present may conclude his or her study with the recitation of the Rabbis' Kaddish. This text glorifies God and asks God's protection "upon Israel, upon the teachers, their disciples and all of their disciples and upon all those who engage in the study of Torah ..." In many congregations, it has become a custom only for those who are mourners or for those who are observing the *yahrzeit*, the anniversary of a loved one's death, to say the Rabbis' Kaddish. Therefore, it is included on the CD.

For his suggestion of the CD of the Kaddish and for his support of *The Kaddish Minyan*, I thank Dan Kahn.

Generous support of this book has been given by the Ben Teitel Trust administered by Jerry Cook. By enthusiastically supporting *The Kaddish Minyan*, Mr. Cook has helped many people in the midst of their grief to be comforted.

Additional contributions were made by Larry Wolfe, president of Adat Shalom Synagogue, Milton J. Miller, Ed Rosenberg, and David Schostak. For their confidence in me and in this book, I thank them.

I thank my dear friends Rabbi Samuel Stahl, who read and critiqued each of the additions in this volume, and Dr. Michael Gellis, who facilitated and introduced the Kaddish on the disc included in this book.

My appreciation goes to my associates Charlotte Fiszbein and Sheila Lederman for typing drafts of the essays added to the second edition.

To the contributors to the first edition as well as to the second expanded edition, I applaud you for the help that you continue to give to others who are walking or will walk through the same valley as you did. May they receive the healing that can come from your words.

—Rabbi Herbert A. Yoskowitz
Farmington Hills, Michigan
April 2003

# Mourner's Kaddish

*Mourners and those observing Yahrzeit:*

יִתְגַּדַּל וְיִתְקַדַּשׁ שְׁמֵהּ רַבָּא. בְּעָלְמָא דִּי בְרָא כִרְעוּתֵהּ, וְיַמְלִיךְ מַלְכוּתֵהּ בְּחַיֵּיכוֹן וּבְיוֹמֵיכוֹן וּבְחַיֵּי דְכָל בֵּית יִשְׂרָאֵל. בַּעֲגָלָא וּבִזְמַן קָרִיב וְאִמְרוּ אָמֵן:

*Congregation and mourners:*

יְהֵא שְׁמֵהּ רַבָּא מְבָרַךְ לְעָלַם וּלְעָלְמֵי עָלְמַיָּא׃

*Mourners:*

יִתְבָּרַךְ וְיִשְׁתַּבַּח, וְיִתְפָּאַר וְיִתְרוֹמַם וְיִתְנַשֵּׂא וְיִתְהַדָּר וְיִתְעַלֶּה וְיִתְהַלָּל שְׁמֵהּ דְּקֻדְשָׁא בְּרִיךְ הוּא לְעֵלָּא מִן כָּל בִּרְכָתָא וְשִׁירָתָא, תֻּשְׁבְּחָתָא וְנֶחֱמָתָא, דַּאֲמִירָן בְּעָלְמָא, וְאִמְרוּ אָמֵן:
יְהֵא שְׁלָמָא רַבָּא מִן שְׁמַיָּא וְחַיִּים עָלֵינוּ וְעַל כָּל יִשְׂרָאֵל, וְאִמְרוּ אָמֵן:
עֹשֶׂה שָׁלוֹם בִּמְרוֹמָיו הוּא יַעֲשֶׂה שָׁלוֹם עָלֵינוּ וְעַל כָּל יִשְׂרָאֵל, וְאִמְרוּ אָמֵן:

# Transliteration of Mourner's Kaddish

*Mourners and those observing Yahrzeit:*
Yit-ga-dal ve-yit-ka-dash She-may raba. (*Amen*)
b'al-ma dee ve-ra khee-re-oo-tay
ve-yam-likh mal-khoo-tay
be-ha-yeh-khon oo-ve-yo-may-khon oo-ve-kha-yay
    de-khol bayt Yis-ra-el
ba-a'-ga-la oo-viz-man ka-riv. Ve-ee-me-roo Amen.

*Congregation and mourners:*
(*Ye-hay She-may rab-ba meva-rakh le-a-lam*
    *oo-le-al-may al-may-ya.*)

*Mourners:*
Yit-ba-rakh ve-yish-ta-bakh ve-yit-pa'ar ve-yit-ro-mam
    ve-yit-na-say
ve-yit-ha-dar ve-yit-a-leh ve-yit-ha-lal
She-may de-kood-sha b'rikh Hoo. (*B'rikh Hoo*)
le-ay-la min kol* bir-kha-ta ve-shee-ra-ta
toosh-be-ha-ta ve-ne-he-ma-ta
da-a-mee-ran b'al-ma. Ve-ee-me-roo Amen. (*Amen*)
Ye-hay she-la-ma rab-ba min she-ma-ya ve-ha-yyim
    a-lay-nu ve-al kol Yis-ra-el. Ve-ee-me-roo Amen
    (*Amen*)
O-seh sha-lom bim-ro-mav Hoo ya-a-seh sha-lom
a-lay-noo ve-al kal Yis-ra-el. Ve-ee-me-roo amen.
    (*Amen*)

---

*From Rosh Hashanah to Yom Kippur substitute:
le-ayla le-ay-la mee-kol

# Translation of Mourner's Kaddish

Hallowed and enhanced may He be throughout the world of His own creation. May He cause His sovereignty soon to be accepted, during our life and the life of all Israel. And let us say: Amen.

May He be praised throughout all time.

---

Glorified and celebrated, lauded and worshipped, acclaimed and honored, extolled and exalted may the Holy One be praised beyond all song and psalm, beyond all tributes which mortals can utter. And let us say: Amen.
Let there be abundant peace from Heaven, with life's goodness for us and for all the people Israel.
And let us say: Amen.

He who brings peace to His universe will bring peace to us and to all the people Israel. And let us say: Amen.

---

Our Creator, the King of kings, delights in life. Because of His love for us, and because we are so few, each of us is important in His kingdom. Though we are flesh and blood, we are irreplaceable. When one of the House of Israel dies, there is a loss of glory in His kingdom and His grandeur is diminished. Therefore, members of the House of Israel, all of you who mourn and all of you who remember on this day, let us fix our hearts on our Father in Heaven, our King and our Redeemer, and let us pray for ourselves, and for Him too, that He and His sovereignty be hallowed and enhanced, glorified and celebrated.

(Reprinted from *Siddur Sim Shalom*, edited by Rabbi Jules Harlow, pages 524-525. Copyright by The Rabbinical Assembly, 1985. Reprinted by permission of The Rabbinical Assembly.)

*"The Jewish way of mourning has turned
an absence into a presence."*

—from Leon Wieseltier's *The Kaddish*

# I.

## INTRODUCTION
By Rabbi Herbert A. Yoskowitz

## Why Kaddish? The Impetus for This Book

The Kaddish evokes a stronger emotional response in Jews than any other prayer in our liturgy. It is recited evening, morning, and afternoon by Jews all over the world; by the richest and the humblest; by the young and the old; by the sophisticated and the simple. Some Jews who otherwise do not adhere to other Jewish traditions faithfully say the Kaddish for eleven months after a parent dies and subsequently during each year on the parent's *yahrzeit.*

Yet, with all the recitation of the Kaddish, to most the Kaddish is shrouded in mystery. Many people in the congregation ask about the Kaddish: its origin, meaning and custom. In response to the many queries, we realized the need to formally present a series of programs on this meaningful prayer.

The programs were well received. In particular, one session had a profound impact on those who attended. At this session I introduced the subject and the panel of mourners, three still in their year of mourning and one who had just completed his eleven months of saying Kaddish. The four of them and I spoke. They were mourning the death of a child, of a parent, and of a spouse. Their words touched the souls of those in attendance.

1

In addition, funeral directors were invited to share taped messages on "The Impact of Kaddish," excerpts of which were shared after the panel of mourners spoke.

One member of the congregation who could not be present contributed her comments after the panel presentations. At a later time, two other congregants and a non-congregant who heard about our program contributed their comments about the impact of Kaddish on them. Colleagues of mine at Adat Shalom Synagogue added their perspectives on the Kaddish.

This book provides a brief introduction to the Kaddish and an appreciation of what the Kaddish can do for the mourner during the required period of saying Kaddish. Its uniqueness lies in the personal views of those who have experienced the phenomena of saying Kaddish. The power of life stories is that we see ourselves in others. When people cope with the ultimate boundary of this life—that is, death—we can be strengthened as we experience our own grief. We are not alone but are a part of a community that shares the universal experience of death. Our own fears are echoed in memories, hopes and prayers.

To read how others utilize Kaddish to help them during their grief is reassuring for our own journey. Their messages of the impact of Kaddish on the mourner are more powerful than anything a Rabbi, "the defender of the faith," can offer. When congregants attest to the power of Kaddish in their lives, a powerful message is broadcast. We are indebted to all those who shared their innermost feelings about their grief and about the impact of the Mourner's Kaddish on them.

It is my hope that the sharing of the experiences in this book will motivate mourners to say Kaddish to honor their deceased relatives and to support their journey of grief, remembrance and healing.

# A Brief Introduction
# to the Kaddish Prayer

While the Kaddish is thought to be a prayer for the dead, essentially it is an affirmation of life. Neither death nor the dead is mentioned.

Originally Kaddish was a response recited at the close of a Rabbinic lesson in the synagogue during the Talmudic Period (200 BCE–550 CE). A message of comfort and consolation would conclude the Rabbi's lesson. Kaddish extended that message by focusing on our messianic hope. This Kaddish is called the Rabbis' Kaddish.

In post-Talmudic time, saying the Kaddish was extended from the House of Study to the House of Prayer and ultimately to the cemetery. The Rabbis taught that Kaddish should be recited for eleven months for a deceased parent. For other deceased relatives, there was a thirty-day obligation to say Kaddish. Today, some choose to say Kaddish for eleven months in memory not just of parents but of other relatives, too.

Kaddish, an Aramaic word for "holy," praises God's name and must be said in public assembly, which is defined as a quorum of at least ten Jewish adults, a *minyan*. In addition to the Rabbi's Kaddish, other forms of Kaddish said during a religious service include the Full Kaddish recited at the end of a service, the Half Kaddish said at the conclusion of smaller prayer units, and the Mourner's Kaddish.

Kaddish is said subsequently by a mourner on the anniversary of the death (*yahrzeit*) of a loved one during all services on that day and on Yom Kippur, Succot, Pesach, and

3

Shavuot when the Memorial Service (Yizkor) is recited. On the *yahrzeit*, it is customary for the mourner to receive an *aliyah*, an honor involving being called to the Torah and reciting Torah blessings expressing joyous sentiments. It is suggested that if the *yahrzeit* occurs on a non-Torah reading day, the person observing the *yahrzeit* should receive an *aliyah* (an opportunity to praise God while standing before the open Torah) in the synagogue on the Shabbat before the *yahrzeit*.

## Some of the Laws of Kaddish

Unsurpassed in Jewish law as a paean to God, the laws of Kaddish are of interest even to Jews who are otherwise indifferent to other aspects of Jewish observance.

The laws of Kaddish instruct us regarding basic questions, such as for whom do we say Kaddish, when may Kaddish be recited, for how long is Kaddish recited. There are more esoteric questions, such as how many times a day should a mourner say Kaddish, and must a son who bears a grudge against his deceased father say Kaddish for him, and under what circumstance may a person be paid to say kaddish? Here is a selection of laws that reflect our tradition's approach:

- Kaddish is required to be said for anyone for whom a mourner sits Shiva*: mother, father, son, daughter, husband, wife, brother and sister.

- Kaddish is recited for a parent for eleven months. For all other relatives for whom Kaddish is required, Kaddish is said for *Shloshim*, thirty days. People may elect to

---

*Shiva is the obligatory seven-day mourning period that immediately follows burial.

say Kaddish for other relatives and for friends, though it is customary not to say Kaddish for such people while parents are alive.

- Only if a religious quorum (*minyan*) is present may one say Kaddish. If no *minyan* is present, the mourner should study a Jewish text in honor of the deceased but not recite the Kaddish. That study can be considered to be an act of sanctification.

- We are cautioned against saying the Mourner's Kaddish excessively. As one medieval Rabbi wrote, "I clamor against those who multiply the recitation of the Mourner's Kaddish any place and any time."

- A child who bears a grudge against a parent is required nonetheless to say Kaddish for that parent. To refrain from doing so reflects unfavorably not only on the memory of a parent but upon the child, too, and may hinder his/her ability to mourn—even to mourn the kind of parent she/he may not have had.

- Similarly, a child may ignore a parent's wish that Kaddish not be recited for the parent.

- If a deceased person has no relatives to recite Kaddish for him or for her, someone should be hired to say the Kaddish. The person saying the Kaddish should say these words before the prayer service begins, "All the Kaddishim I recite today are for the benefit of the soul of (name of the deceased)." Then he adds the words of Psalm 90:17: "May the favor of the Lord, our God, be upon us; let the work of our hands prosper, O prosper the work of our hands."

Consult your own Rabbinic authority with particular questions or concerns about saying Kaddish.

# The Kaddish and Immortality

The Kaddish does not mention death. Instead, the words focus on God's majesty, magnificence and sanctity. However, one Rabbinic story that is repeated many times in midrashic lore links the Kaddish to the souls of the deceased.

Rabbi Akiva walked near a graveyard and saw the soul (or spirit) of someone who had died. That soul was restless and disturbed. "Who are you," Rabbi Akiva asked, "and what have you done?"

The man said, "The man whom you are addressing is a dead man. Every day they send me out to chop wood."

"My son, what was your work in the world from which you came?"

"I was a tax collector, and I would favor the rich and kill the poor."

"Have your superiors told you nothing about how you might relieve your condition?"

"Please, sir, do not detain me, for you will irritate my tormentors. For such a man (as I), there can be no relief. Though I did hear them say something—but no, it is impossible. They said that if this poor man had a son, and his son were to stand before the congregation and recite (the prayer) 'Bless the Lord who is blessed!' and the congregation were to answer amen, and the son were also to say 'May the Great Name be blessed!' (a sentence from the Kaddish), they would release him from his punishment." (Wieseltier: *Kaddish*, page 41)

Thus, the Kaddish said by a child for a deceased parent is thought to improve the life of the immortal soul of the parent in the world-to-come. Additionally, the lives of all the souls in the world-to-come are thought to be improved when Kaddish is recited for them collectively, such as when Kaddish is said for the Six Million or when Kaddish is recited for a specific deceased person. We say the Kaddish for loved ones who are in the world-to-come, and we bring their memories to mind in a heightened manner.

However, the world-to-come is described in Jewish sources, with its many and varied interpretations, as being tied to the hopes of the arrival of the Messianic period and of the resurrection of the dead.

The Messianic Era is part of the hope of what will happen after the physical life is ended. Healing the world—*Tikkun Olam*—is connected to the days of the Messiah. Healing the world, one of the strongest injunctions in Judaism, actually mirrors the ultimate Jewish hope for the afterlife.

The Kaddish gives us a hint of this connection. The Kaddish asks for the hastening of the day when the earth reflects Godliness. It describes a world in which God's perfection and the praises of God's name are so evident that God's world and the world on which human history unfolds become the same. It affirms the possibility of healing the world and calls for the peace of "God's high place" to be known here on earth. The goal of the Kaddish, in fact, is to bring together the two worlds of *Olam Hazeh*, our present existence, and *Olam Haba*, which in its ultimate form is the Messianic Era.

While resurrection of the dead in the distant future is usually interpreted as the bodily reconstitution of the deceased individual, it is depicted as the collective national revival of the entire Jewish people, too. Resurrection has come closest to acquiring the status of dogma in Jewish tradition. In the synagogue on Friday nights, it is sung in the concluding article of the thirteen articles of the *Yigdal* hymn, based on the creed of Maimonides and in the daily Amidah.

Maimonides' creed notwithstanding, there is no clearly

7

iterated dogmatic position regarding what happens after we complete our physical life. There is a melding of many components in the eschatological visions across the ages and through to the present day.

Until that Messianic Era arrives, our Kaddish prayer links us to the souls of our beloved whether we believe in the literal hope of the resurrection, which ties body and soul together as an inseparable spirit, or in the figurative interpretation that the immortal soul has a separate existence from the mortal body.

The Kaddish is clearly linked to our conviction that our souls are immortal. The souls of those who have died continue to influence our own souls; our spiritual relationship does not end because the body is no longer present and alive among us.

## Remembrances

With the end of the eleven-month period following burial, the most intensive rites that have permeated the lives of the mourners are brought to a close. However, the persistence and healing value of human memory necessitates some continuing form of recognition of a loss of a loved one. From this point on, the deceased are ritually remembered on five occasions during the year: They are the *yahrzeit*, as well as the four holidays when *yizkor* is said: Yom Kippur, Passover, Shavuot, and Shemini Atzeret. *Yahrzeit* and *yizkor* observance are later developments, probably dating from the Middle Ages. *Yahrzeit* is a Yiddish word of German origin, and Jews didn't speak Yiddish until the latter sixteenth to early seventeenth century, for the most part.

On the day of the *yahrzeit*, a memorial candle ought to be lit, charitable acts should be performed, and Jewish study should be included. Some people have even fasted on the *yahrzeit* of one's parents. They also visit the grave site and recite Psalms such as the ones often recited at an unveiling: Psalms 8, 19, 23, 46, 104, 120, 139, 146.

Beginning in the late nineteenth century, *yahrzeit* calendars were printed in Israel, Europe, and the United States. While the *yahrzeit* falls on the same day according to the Jewish calendar, its secular date varies from year to year. Contact your rabbi or chaplain for help in calculating the dates. The *yahrzeit* remains an important point of contact with Jewish tradition, even for Jewish people who may not be observant in other areas of Jewish life.

## Leon Wieseltier's Kaddish Experience

A work about Kaddish is the highly acclaimed book *Kaddish* by Leon Wieseltier (published in 1998 by Knopf). When Leon Wieseltier's father died, Leon undertook to recite the Mourner's Kaddish at public worship three times a day. He did so for eleven months.

Wieseltier tells the story of the eleven months of saying Kaddish and of all his studies about Kaddish during those eleven months. The author reflects upon the great issues of life and death considered through the prisms of memory and of grief. Wieseltier enters into a dialogue with the great Judaic intellects of the ages whom he knows as companions. The result is a profound work not merely about Judaism but of Judaism.

Wieseltier enlists erudition to give comfort to the soul. He voices a controlled despair and restraint by saying Kaddish and by studying comments made about Kaddish by Jews over the period of many centuries.

Regarding the constancy of the author's rendition of Kaddish three times a day in a *minyan*, he writes that his unexpected fidelity to this obscure and arduous practice turned a season of sorrow into a season of soul renovation. Raised in a traditional Jewish home, Wieseltier moved away from religious observance as an adult. "Why," a friend asked, "did he choose to say Kaddish?" His answer is straightforward and compelling:

> Because it is my duty to my father. Because it is my duty to religion. . . . Because it would be harder for me not to say Kaddish. I would despise myself. Because the fulfillment of my duty leaves my thoughts about my father unimpeded by regret and undistorted by guilt.

Wieseltier establishes close bonds with the mourners in his synagogue. He is forever on the run between his office and the synagogue, not only because he is saying Kaddish, but *because there are other mourners to whom he feels obligated*. Similarly there is always someone else at the synagogue ready to make phone calls to gather a *minyan* so that Wieseltier can say Kaddish. Newcomers who appear on the scene are warmly welcomed whatever their background. Wieseltier writes:

> The Rabbi introduces me to two men. They are brothers and they buried their father this morning. They have come to say Kaddish but they are not familiar with the words and the customs of the prayer. The Rabbi asks me to help. Soon it is time to recite the Kaddish. The brothers rise with me.
> They read a transliteration of the prayer: "We are the dunces," one of them says. "No," I reply, "the dunces are the ones who don't try." As I watched the brothers struggle with the transliterated prayer, I admired them. The sounds that they uttered made no sense to them but there was so much fidelity, so much humility, in their gibberish.

Eleven months is a long time. On some mornings, Wieseltier struggles to rise at an early morning hour to go to the synagogue. As his eleven months of saying Kaddish

10

enters the final stretch, he is frightened at the prospect of finishing. "As the end of the Kaddish nears," he states openly, "I am scared." And he explains why.

> For as long as I have been organizing my life around the Kaddish, I have been organizing my life around my father. When Kaddish is over, he will be gone. My strict observance of the year of mourning has had a consequence of delaying the return of a normal life. I have lived in a state of suspension, shielded from a fatherless world by a father-full practice. The Jewish way of mourning has turned an absence into a presence.

At times during the eleven months, Wieseltier wonders why he is saying Kaddish. He is making a dedicated effort to say Kaddish even though he never made that kind of effort to see his father when he was alive. Wieseltier affirms, *"Our fathers did not have the authority to ask this of us but our religion does."* He is saying Kaddish to help himself deal with the impact that his grieving has on him. He continues to say Kaddish for the year.

Wieseltier, a great writer, has expressed himself very well regarding the Kaddish. You will find, as I have already found, that the people whose words you are about to read have also expressed themselves well about the impact of the Kaddish on them. They speak from the heart in a way that can move you.

# II.

## THE IMPACT OF GRIEVING AND THE IMPORTANCE OF SAYING KADDISH: TWENTY VOICES

### In Memory of My Father
By Benson J. Barr

My father's death was not a singular event. Instead, Alzheimer's Disease, in its inexorable process, forced us to watch the process of death almost as if it were in stop action—a slow-motion movie. As each element of his unique being was taken from him, those of us who loved him watched, paused with pain and grief, and moved on. We tried our best to be encouraging and supportive, both of our father (whose very being seemed to be slowly disappearing) and of our mother, who so loyally cared for him.

There is no prescribed ritual to mourn the incremental deaths of a loved one (through a long-term chronic disease, such as Alzheimer's). As each small element of the person's personality or physical ability is destroyed and gone forever, there is no prayer of which I am aware to signify the loss. What can be said or how does one react when a father no longer can distinguish between a spoon, fork or knife, or no longer can read, draw, write or play the violin, or remember the members of his own family for whom his love was boundless?

13

When he died, I began to attend morning services with a fair amount of skepticism, not having been a particularly observant Jew in the past. I was not sure whether I would attend for more than a week or so. I was embarrassed by the fact that I had forgotten how to put on *tefillin*. I was not sure how the services would fit into my schedule. It was not clear to me that participation in the daily services would provide emotional solace or have a spiritual effect on me. However, as time passed, the reasons that I was in attendance on a daily basis began to crystallize.

Kaddish has provided a mechanism to mourn and to recognize the passage of my father's life. Furthermore, it provides a time in the day to recognize his life and death without the disruptions that occur in each of our lives during an ordinary day.

Leon Wieseltier wrote: "A friend asked why I am saying Kaddish. A good question. These were my answers. Because it is my duty to my father. Because it is my duty to my religion. (These are the strong reasons; the non-utilitarian reasons.) Because it would be harder not to say Kaddish. (I would despise myself.) Because the fulfillment of my duty leaves my thoughts about my father unimpeded by regret and undistorted by guilt. On the subject of fathers and sons, my chore keeps me clear."[1]

One of the ironies of Alzheimer's Disease is that it not only steals the memory of the person afflicted; it also dulls and fades the memories of the family members that were built over a lifetime before the onset of the disease. It is ironic how a full and vigorous life of years can be obscured by seven years of disease.

Kaddish enables me to remember my father, not only in the last years of his mental decline, but also in those many decades of his vitality and strength.

Kaddish also provides a routine and focus to the mourning/grieving process that might otherwise be chaotic or without form. I cannot tell my brain when to have thoughts of my father and my life with him, but I can seek to concentrate and focus on those thoughts during the daily service. "... Kaddish is my good fortune. It looks after the externals, and so it saves me from the task of improvising the rituals of my bereavement, which is a lot to ask."[2]

Finally, Kaddish demonstrates to my children the importance that I place on our Jewish tradition and the respect and honor that I desire to bestow upon the memory of my father. I can only expect my children to honor me if I continue to demonstrate to them that I honor my own father in death, as I did during his life. To expect otherwise would be presumptuous.

---

1. Leon Wieseltier, *Kaddish* (New York: Alfred A. Knopf, 1998), pp. 25–26.
2. *Ibid.*, p. 39.

# Belonging, Behaving, Perhaps Even Believing

By Irving Berman

Before my father's death, my daily worship was nonexistent. My attendance at synagogue fell into the category of yearly. When I wished the clergy a good year, it was because, outside of a wedding or Bar Mitzvah, that was the next time I was likely to see them.

After the Shiva period ended, I was faced with living up to the commitment I had made to my father to say Kaddish for him. The reading of the Kaddish at three services each day seemed like a chore that was monumental. The first time I attended the morning service, I had little knowledge of what lay ahead. I was "doing this" for my dad. That first morning I was greeted by some of the "regulars" and found I had gained admittance to a club that none of us had wanted to join. My Hebrew skills were "rusty" to say the least. I was happy just to know what page we were on and when to stand and sit. For the next eleven months, and the first time in my adult life, my religion was to become a conscious part of my daily regimen.

As the days went by, I began to understand the purpose of the Kaddish service and feel its effect on me. I thought about my father every day. I began and ended my day with a peaceful meditation and "conversation" with my God. I took time, not only for my father, but also for myself. Some of the mystery surrounding prayers, holidays, and traditions began to disappear. I met with other Jews who were attending services, out of necessity or by choice. I even found my

16

"barely used" *t'fillin* [phylacteries] and began using them. I felt the healing process begin, and found that I was gaining a new and personal relationship with my religion. What had started out as a chore had become a satisfying task. What was once something I did for my father was now something I did for the two of us.

During the course of the eleven months, the members of the "club" changed. Each of us gained as much as we wanted. My Hebrew reading skills improved so that I was able to keep up with the service. I celebrated holidays and attended services that I had not participated in since I was a child. I even attended some services that I had never heard of before. My effort to fulfill my daily Kaddish obligations took so much of my time and energy that I did not realize how soothing an impact it was having on me. The eleven months that at first seemed like an eternity passed in the blink of an eye. The loss that I felt I would never get over resulted in a life experience I now look at with a sense of pride. I learned a tremendous amount about my religion, met some wonderful people and found out a lot about myself. The last day, after saying my final required Kaddish, I stood on the *bimah* and led Maariv, the evening service. I was now doing it for me.

The Kaddish experience acted not only as a healing exercise, but a strengthening bond between myself, my father, my grandfather and those who preceded them. I am more aware that there is more to being Jewish than Bris [ritual circumcision of boys at the age of eight days], Bar Mitzvah, and burial. A great deal is available in between, if we take the time to look for it.

# A Personal Obligation to My Daughter's Memory

By George Cantor

My eighteen-year-old daughter died in the fall of 1998. She fell from her sixth-floor dormitory window at the University of Michigan. We still don't know how or why. All I knew with certainty was that Courtney's death filled me with a sense of anger and futility.

We had raised a bright, funny, beautiful young woman. We watched with delight as her Jewish awareness grew after a summer spent in Israel. We rejoiced with her when the acceptance from Ann Arbor came through. We planned with her for the big move.

And in an instant, it was over. Where was the meaning, the sense to it? I had always considered myself an optimist, and this shattered every conviction I ever had about the assurance of the future.

I told myself that I had a fulfilling career. A loving wife. A brilliant daughter who would soon enter Harvard Law School. Parents who were still vital and happy into their eighties.

None of it mattered. If this could happen, what was the point of the whole thing? I had a rather serious quarrel with the Almighty and, like any decent journalist, wanted some answers.

I was raised in the Conservative tradition, but my wife's family had been founding members of a large reform congregation. This is where she felt comfortable and that is where we became members.

I thought it was important to set a good example for my daughters in religious matters. In my mind, that consisted of sending them to Sunday school and Confirmation classes and of attending services on the High Holidays. Other observances were done out of habit rather than any sense of conviction. The concept that my religion could be a source of solace and healing was not part of the deal.

I knew, however, that I would say Kaddish for Courtney for the traditional full eleven months, even though the requirement technically was only for one month for the loss of a child. To me, this was an unshakable personal obligation to my daughter's memory. What I never foresaw was that it would also restore my wife and me to life.

Temple Israel holds morning services five days a week. The *minyan* group sits around a large table in the Temple library, with the leader at its head. On Sunday mornings, it can draw as many as three dozen people, but on weekdays the usual turnout is about fifteen.

I didn't know what to expect and had some trepidation about the whole thing. I knew some of the people in the group only slightly. Most I had never met. But I soon learned that we were not strangers.

We were a self-selected group of Jews who had chosen to turn away from our assimilated lives to satisfy the requirements of our religion. We actually knew each other well. To my surprise, my wife also began coming to the service, and despite being unable to read Hebrew, she became an enthusiastic participant.

As time went on, we lingered after services to share our stories and our grief, to talk about what we were going through and, occasionally, to cry. Members of our *minyan* are now among our closest friends.

We also had the certain knowledge that we had joined with other Jews, living and dead, who had come together in sorrow for centuries to reaffirm their faith by reciting these

19

same prayers. We were fortified by their company and, eventually, encouraged to take a more active role in Jewish life.

The pain of losing our daughter will never go away. I understand that. I don't think it's supposed to. But out of this immeasurable loss, we have gained as human beings and made a new commitment to live a life of Jewish values.

The Kaddish brought us home.

# Reciting Kaddish at an Orthodox Minyan: A Daughter's Thanks and Memories

By Tamy S. Chelst, Ph.D.

I thank those who prayed with me in the daily *minyan* for the consideration and respect they showed to a woman who joined the daily prayers during the past year that I said Kaddish in memory of my dear mother. I also thank the rabbis for welcoming me and for supporting a woman mourner's halachic role in saying Kaddish.

Now that the first *yahrzeit* has occurred, I have to reflect on what we have learned together, as I joined others daily to pray. The predominantly male daily *minyan* learned to accept women as regular worshipers and to answer "*yehei shemei rabba*" to my voice.

What did the *minyan* have to gain by my presence? Who needed a female participant, especially when one female does not add to the much needed magical number "ten" that allows the congregants to pray as a unit? To begin with, because men count, I often brought numbers nine and ten; i.e., my husband and my youngest son.

The rabbi or guest speaker who commonly learn during evening prayers gained one more person actually to listen to what they had to say. In addition, I supported those whose prayer recitation was at a moderate, rather than a hurried, pace.

I urge people to pay more attention to the social aspects of saying Kaddish. If someone were to ask me what women mourners can contribute during the year of Kaddish, I feel

21

that it is the highlighting among the mourners of shared emotional support and shared life experiences. Saying the prayer daily is not only a personal cathartic for the mourner who is working through his/her grief; it is also an opportunity to share the life experiences of a mourner.

I well remember the visit of a young woman from Toronto, who joined me on two occasions for several days of saying Kaddish while she cleaned her mother's home and cared for the details of her estate. We had much information and support to share with one another. What to do with the car? How to sell the furnishings? How to share tasks with other siblings in order not to feel overburdened?

The men in our *shul* can also utilize this social support system. They may find assistance from a sharing of information and a pacing of mutual experiences after the loss of a parent.

There is a praying mode that is established in the Kaddish year. Mourners often feel that they want to continue their daily attendance, even after the eleven or twelve months. That same young woman who visited in Detroit wrote:

> "I felt at the end of the eleven months that I was not yet ready to be 'finished' with going to *shul*. I found myself at a perplexing cross road, especially considering family responsibilities. After a *she'elah* (question) was answered, it turned out that although I no longer could say Kaddish Yatom, Kaddish d'Rabbanan (the Kaddish after learning a Jewish text with a quorum) was, in fact, permissible."

Kaddish is said to comfort the soul of the deceased. A son or daughter, by virtue of his or her piety, may exert influence in heaven on behalf of a deceased parent. My mother lived in my home for the last five years of her life and in Detroit for the last ten years. I am grateful to the *Kaddish minyan* for allowing me another eleven months to continue with her daily care.

# Worth the Effort

By Dr. Ronald Fogel

Although my mother had been valiantly coping with a chronic illness for many years, her sudden deterioration and subsequent death came as a shock to us all. During the two months that she lay comatose, there was no opportunity for any of us to come to terms with her life or to accept her impending death. On an intellectual level, as a physician, my goal is to alleviate suffering. Yet emotionally, accepting that there was nothing to be done for my mother, I felt powerless and vulnerable.

Because I had been a regular attendee at services and always found comfort in Judaism, I decided that it would be important for me to honor my mother by saying Kaddish. To me, this meant attending all three daily services. When I made this choice, I had no idea whether saying Kaddish would be meaningful in providing spirituality and healing or whether the commitment would result in frustration and anxiety, as I struggled to juggle my professional schedule and family responsibilities with synagogue attendance.

Looking back, the months of saying Kaddish were a burden which was physically and emotionally exhausting. I was always tired. There was a demoralizing sameness to each day and a uniformity to the weeks and months. Saying Kaddish became the focus of my activities. Controlling my day's activities became impossible, because all plans were based on the timing of services. My work day was shortened. I was either arriving late from morning service or leaving early to attend

23

afternoon/evening prayers. I was always looking at the clock, deciding which tasks could be done prior to leaving for *Mincha/Ma'ariv* services and which must be postponed to the next day. I was always rushing, always planning how I could get to the next service.

Traveling became a logistical nightmare. Before any trip, calls were made to synagogues to learn the schedule of services and the best directions to the synagogue from hotel or meeting center. Flights had to be arranged that would allow me to attend my meeting but also to be available for services.

Family activities were planned around services. Everything from the timing of meals to whether I could help our daughter with her move from college was predicated on the time of services.

Was all this physical effort and emotional stress worthwhile? The answer is an unqualified yes. I was provided the opportunity to learn about the importance of a Jewish community. I gained strength from my community and was privileged to experience the generosity and kindness of its members.

Saying Kaddish requires a presence of a community of at least ten. During these last two months, I have met people who changed vacation plans or a day's activities in order to attend services to provide a *minyan*. While in San Francisco, I met a couple on their honeymoon who happened to walk by a small synagogue while we were looking for a tenth person. Once we spoke, the husband volunteered to be at services every day during his stay to guarantee a *minyan*.

In my own community, after attending services with the same people for several months, I was surprised to realize how much I enjoyed their company and how I looked forward to seeing them each day. Each mourner has a unique story of loss. Because of our common experience, however, we were open to the expressions of sadness, anger, and loss. There was no embarrassment in the sudden shedding of tears or the sentences that could not be completed because the speaker was overtaken with emotion. The opportunity to provide comfort, as well as to receive support, had a powerful healing effect.

Although the Kaddish does not directly address the issue of death, the act of standing and saying the Mourner's Kaddish marks one publicly as an individual who has suffered a loss. There is a surreal quality of standing in the sanctuary and hearing one's own voice, saying the words slowly and deliberately. The experience forced me to remember my mother. In the first months, my mind raced, as I relived the happy occasions and then the suffering of the final illness. However, over the months, this experience became less intense. Amazingly, I did not feel as if I were losing my mother again. Saying Kaddish each day was our connection.

The Kaddish is a bond that links the generations. My congregation of mourners were at different ages and different stages of life and had experienced unique relationships with the subjects of their loss. Saying Kaddish linked us to another generation and anchored us in our time.

# Compassionate Club
## By Andrea Gordon

Monday morning, 7:35 A.M. There are approximately thirty people seated here and there around the small chapel. One of the clergy says the word, "Kaddish," and many of us rise.

*Yitgadal v'yitkadash sh'mei raba*

I'm wearing a black ribbon with a tear in it.

*b'alma di v'ra khir'utei, v'yamlikh malkhutei*

I'm no longer part of the group with two living parents. For the next eleven months, I will stand in *shul* and recite this prayer with others who have suffered a loss in their family.

*b'hayeikhon u-v'yomeikhon u-v'hayei d'khol beit yisrael,*

Yesterday, I buried my mother. Last night I began to say Kaddish. Now it is Monday morning, only twenty-one hours since the funeral.

*. . . ba-agala u-vi-z'man kariv v'imru amen.*

Tears. I can't speak. I can barely focus on the page in front of me. I am reciting Kaddish in my mind, but no sound is coming from my throat.

26

My mother died on Friday morning at 1:00 A.M. She had been very ill for two years, and her deteriorating condition had been painful to watch. Before that, she had been full of life and busy doing all kinds of wonderful things for her family and community.

The funeral was scheduled for Sunday morning. On Saturday night, we waited for my sister and her family to fly in to Detroit from California. We had agreed that we would sit Shiva at my home and hold evening services here every night during that week. We knew, however, that we would not be able to gather a *minyan* each morning, so for the mornings of Shiva, my Dad, brother, sisters, and I met at *shul* for morning *minyan*.

That first Monday morning was difficult. My experience at *shul* over the past five decades was associated with joyous occasions, like Shabbat services or Holiday services or religious school programs. I had been going to *shul* since I was a baby. My four children accompanied me to *shul* from the time that they began to walk. Standing for Kaddish was foreign to me. Yes, I knew the prayer by heart, but Kaddish was for my parents and others who had lost someone to say. I always stayed seated when they stood up for Kaddish. On Holidays, when Yizkor was said, I walked out of the Main Sanctuary to talk with my friends. Now all of a sudden, I was no longer a member of that elite group who were not required to say Kaddish and never would be again.

The only time I felt comfort that first morning at *shul* was when our two rabbis at different points in the service came over to me and briefly expressed their condolences. Near the end of the service, I suddenly realized the cantor had come over to do the same thing. Those were nice gestures.

Someone invited me to stay for breakfast. What a novel idea! I hardly ever had time to eat breakfast. My mornings were full, with the usual routine of any family when trying to get children off to school. Usually, by the time I had com-

27

pleted briefly reviewing the lesson plans for my classes, there was no time for me to sit and to eat breakfast. But now everything was different. My husband took over the morning routine at home so that I could go to *shul*. Since I don't have to be in my classroom until 9:00 A.M. and services end at 8:15 A.M., there was time for *Motzi* (the prayer praising God for bread), breakfast, and *Birkat* (the grace after meals). But it was difficult to eat, hard to swallow, hard not to cry. Yet everyone around me was understanding, kind, quiet, supportive.

The rest of the week at *shul* was difficult. Tears came easily. I used a lot of Kleenex. I became acquainted with a few of the women. They asked me whom I had lost, and I told them, "My mother." How hard it was to say that! They nodded in sympathy and said, "That's the way life is." We talked. They were so compassionate.

On Friday night, my family came with me to *shul*. It was crowded, hardly an empty seat anywhere. At a certain point in the service, we and other new mourners still in their week of Shiva were ushered out into the hall, and a short time later, we were welcomed back into the fold, after the last stanza of "Lekha Dodi," welcoming the Shabbat, was sung. My mother's name was mentioned along with those of the others who had passed away that week. What a sad Friday night! When I stood up to recite Kaddish, I was shocked by the volume of the people in the small Shiffman Chapel, saying the responsive line, "Y'hei sh' mei raba m'vorakh l'alam u-l'almei almaya." It sounded thunderous. I looked around and realized what a wonderful support group this was. I felt shored up by their presence.

I decided to continue coming to the morning *minyan*. The second week for me was sprinkled with tears, but I became more familiar with the service and could find my way in the prayer book more easily. It was starting to feel right.

By the beginning of the third week, many of the regulars

began coming over to wish me a good morning at the end of services and to talk with me. What a warm, kind, friendly group! I hadn't noticed this before. I had been too wrapped up in my pain.

I'm into the routine now. It feels normal to start my morning at *shul*. *Shloshim* will end in seven more days, but I will continue to come for the full eleven months. I am comfortable here in our small Shiffman Chapel. Sadly, there will be many others this year who will join us to say Kaddish for a loved one. That's the way life is.

The *Kaddish minyan* is so incredible! I will be there to help the next person, and the next, because I know how it feels to be comforted by the *Kaddish minyan*. After all, I am now a member of a very compassionate club.

# Pulled Up and Pulled In

By Bill Graham

Ten months ago, our seventeen-year-old daughter, Alex, died of cancer. We had no regrets, as we did everything that could be done to save her life. We had no guilt, no anger and we were at peace.

Statistically I am significantly different from most members of the congregation. I keep kosher at home and out, virtually never miss Shabbat services, and lay *t'fillin* six days per week. Except for the period that our daughter was sick, I attended morning services once a week to help to assure that there would be a *minyan* so that others could say Kaddish. Saying Kaddish certainly hasn't been a life-changing event.

My first experience of saying Kaddish occurred nine years ago when my father died. He was a *mensch* [a gentleman], but not a spiritual person, and he was not Jewish. When a Jew mourns for a non-Jew, there are several opinions. Generally the process ends up being a compromise among the various siblings. I chose to be with my relatives until the funeral and then to say Kaddish at my synagogue for the *Shloshim* only.

After our daughter died, coming to morning services and saying Kaddish was the most natural thing for me to do. It was a way to honor her memory and, more importantly, it was a way for me to reaffirm my faith in God. Depending upon which Rabbi you ask, one should say Kaddish for just the thirty-day *Shloshim* period or for the full eleven months, as we chose to do. I have to be frank with you, I dreaded the thought of having to get up at 6:30 every weekday morning, and be at the synagogue by 7:30 on weekdays, and be committed to this discipline for eleven months. For thirteen months, I was doing everything that I could to save Alex's life and to make her life more normal. When Alex died, I lost a great deal of interest in life. Saying Kaddish took me out of the house and enabled me to be around old friends and to meet new friends.

Initially on days when the Torah was read, I just wanted to sit in my seat and not participate. Slowly our cantor urged me to participate by taking out and returning the Torah or by serving as *hagbah* [the person who raises the Torah from the Reading Table after the public reading] and then by receiving an *aliyah*. It could be likened to a very subtle pulling-up ceremony after one completes the *Shiva* period. It was one of the many small steps in returning from my daughter's grave to life. By saying Kaddish for the full eleven months, I avoided the potential for relapsing into seclusion and feeling alone.

Although I know modern Hebrew very well, I find the Aramaic of the Kaddish difficult to enunciate. The Kaddish d'Rabbanan (the Rabbis' Kaddish) is particularly difficult to enunciate, but, as my Rabbi says, "There is something special about the Aramaic that has precluded it from ever being translated into a more modern Hebrew." I agree.

If you ever see me at services, you'll notice that I tend to arrive late and have the *spilkas*, an edginess. I tend to find the Small Chapel too warm, so I get up, stand by the window a lot, and almost never stay for breakfast. I miss Alex terribly, but I accept her death as part of the human condition. It's part of the "deal." I am at peace during Kaddish; I feel as if I am a *tallit* [a prayer shawl] and I am wrapping myself around her, giving her comfort. In reality, I know that she is the one who is giving me comfort.

In closing, I say Kaddish as a means of honoring our daughter and gaining comfort, but, most of all, reaffirming my

31

faith in God. It is my faith that has given me the strength these past two years. If it were not for my faith in God, I would never have been able to handle this tragedy.

I have to admit that I'm beginning to have a panic attack. Kaddish will end in a month; I want it to last longer. However, eleven months is enough to say Kaddish. I have a lifetime to cherish the memories and will always have a special place in my heart for Alex.

# Friends in the Small Chapel

## By Susie Graham

Initially Kaddish was a form of respect for my daughter. Ultimately, the final respect. It was hard, at first, to get up so early each morning; the truth is, it was much easier to be in bed and hide. But there was a strong current pulling me along. Throughout my journey over the last nine and a half months, saying the Kaddish has become my salvation. Most of the time, I'm not so sure what I am saying. When I can risk losing my place, I glance over at the English. It's interesting how the Kaddish prayer has nothing to do with death, but rather with praising God. And, in praising God, I think I reaffirm my belief in God at a time when it is so easy to lose faith and certainly question life and everything I once thought to be true. I now ask the question, "What will I do when Kaddish is no longer required of me?"

Saying Kaddish each morning has also somehow connected me with the past. The repetition ... I think of my ancestors repeating the same prayers as I do now. I generally come to the morning service, Shaharit, so that not only am I saying Kaddish, but also observing an eleven-month period of the Jewish calendar! How much I've absorbed! Each morning is the same, yet so different—different people, people also suffering a loss, people remembering a loved one. Celebrations of Bar and Bat Mitzvah. A metaphor for life.

What a learning experience! I've brushed up on my Hebrew. I delight in the melodies. I can follow the service. I actually think of one day leading the service. I help a new friend when she's lost her place. She's lost her husband. She relies on me. Life cycles. Unspoken words. Grief abounds. How close I've become to the Torah, both physically and spiritually. Sometimes I flip through the *siddur* and read Psalms. They console me.

In our large sanctuary on Shabbat morning, interestingly enough, I feel more secluded. My friends are not close to me, as they are in the small chapel. They sit in different sections of the sanctuary, some very far away. It is not as comfortable for me to stand up. Is everyone looking at me? Do they feel sorry for me? I stand with pride as I recite those age-old words.

I am a member of a very prestigious club that I did not choose. My comrades have all been wounded. They acknowledge me with a sweet smile. They understand how fragile life is. They understand my pain as I do theirs. They comfort me as the words of the Kaddish do. I am at peace.

# My Father's Laughter

## By Karen Hermelin

I want to take you back to a little over a year ago, when my father, David Hermelin, was unsuccessfully battling cancer. I was helping him into bed one day, and after fluffing up the pillows and adjusting his back, I asked if he was comfortable. He leaned into me and said weakly, "I make a living." It's a bad joke, but I promise, if he'd been here delivering it, you would have really laughed. He was amazing at making people laugh and communicating profound messages all at the same time.

Unfortunately, my father died a little over a year ago, and the personal journey I'm here to discuss is of the year I spent saying Kaddish for him.

Let me start by saying that one of the many important values my father instilled in his five children, in addition to the love of a good joke, was the love of being Jewish. He was passionate about it, and he was incredibly successful in sharing his passion. I love being Jewish. I am a proud Jew, and I love our culture and heritage. But I must confess: I hated *shul*. Every second of it. So I only went when I had to. Perhaps that's why though I've lived in Los Angeles for eleven years, and am very involved with the Jewish community, I had never joined a *shul*.

But when my dad died, I knew I would say Kaddish for him, twice a day for the full eleven months. Each of us five children made the same decision. We had each witnessed him say the Kaddish, not once or twice, but three times in his life, so we knew how important it was to him.

35

So, after my father died, I went from being a twice-a-year Jew to a twice-a-day Jew. It was a bit of an adjustment.

But this was something I was doing for him. Not for me. I was clear about that.

But now the hard part. At the time, I had a nine-month-old baby, and both my sister and I live on the East Side of town. The closest Jewish community to us is ultra-Orthodox, and the only Conservative synagogues we knew about at the time were on the West Side—too far for a twice-a-day trip.

The first morning, I woke up early, donned my long skirt, and went off to *shul*. Julie and I found ourselves alone behind a *mehitza*, trying in vain to follow the service that sped by without a single page number or word in English being spoken, and just barely able to keep up when the Kaddish was said.

Over time we got better at following the service, but every day, twice a day, for eleven months—we needed something more. Thus began our nomadic survey of synagogues in Los Angeles.

There is no time to go through all the synagogues we visited, but, suffice it to say that by the end of the year, both Julie and I had prayed at nearly twenty different services. We went anywhere that might be interesting or convenient: Reform to Orthodox, Reconstructionist to Conservative. We found a huge and dynamic range of practices within Los Angeles—from beautiful buildings with dying congregations to roving congregations with only passion and spirit to hold them together.

We became experts on who had the most interactive service, the shortest service, the latest start, and the earliest end. We attended all the hot Shabbat services. For a full year, I always kept a long skirt in my car, just in case I had to hop into the nearest Orthodox *minyan*.

Initially, I was surprised to find comfort in setting aside an hour each day to try to regain my lost bearings. But in time, the effort just became a burden, and I was beginning to lose sight even of my dad, in the crush of trying to squeeze in services along with my life.

It was at one service, when I was feeling particularly disconnected, that I consciously decided to close my eyes and think about my dad when I said the Kaddish. Suddenly I saw him, not sick as he had been so often in my memories since his death, but his old self, laughing to see me at *shul* on a Thursday afternoon, as if he were there recognizing the absurdity of it all. It made me laugh out loud in the middle of the service.

But afterward, I thought about it. Was it really the absurdity of me at *shul* on a weekday that made him laugh? Or was he laughing at the fact that this last practical joke he pulled on his kids was really his last great lesson?

After that moment I started to pay attention to how I was really feeling. As I knew it better, the service stopped being so painful and I found a comfort in its rhythm. I found I could seek out new and creative services like this one today that moved me spiritually. I began looking forward to spending Shabbat with familiar faces, and with my daughter at whichever great service I had discovered.

For my daughter, *shul* has become a place she loves in a way I never have. She loves everything about it: the people, the singing, the books, saying "Amen" at the top of her lungs. And it breaks my heart and gives me unbelievable joy that somehow my dad passed this love to my daughter, though he barely had enough time to know her.

And then I remembered being eight and going with my dad to say Kaddish for his mother, and how I loved being in *shul* with him and all the men early in the morning, and how I felt so special. And I realized how that memory had simply been lost in my years of going to cold services that held no meaning for me.

When my last day of Kaddish finally came, I thought I

would be relieved—no more juggling, no more rushing out to *shul* leaving my infinitely understanding husband to care for our child. But after saying the prayer the last time, I broke down. I don't know why, but I cried from the bottom of my soul. Perhaps I wasn't quite ready to stop.

Some say that meaningful traditions last, and those that lose their meaning fall away. Judging by the struggle Conservative synagogues have just to fill a daily *minyan* and by the dearth of young people we saw day to day, it seems that saying the daily Kaddish may be disappearing in the Conservative community, as it already has in much of the Reform. And that would be a shame.

Tradition says that each time the Kaddish is said, it helps the soul of the departed reach its final resting place sooner. But I found that the Jewish mourning ritual is a gift—not just for the dead, but for the living.

Nothing will fill the hole my dad's absence has left in my world. No prayer has provided me with the guidance or answers that he was so brilliant at doing. But what the Kaddish gave me was sacred time to be a *mourner*. Not just for seven days of *shiva*, or those first few weeks when people were giving me their condolences, but every day for a year, I stood up in a room, embraced by community, and identified myself as someone in mourning—which was exactly how I felt. I clearly couldn't live my life that way. But my heart knew my pain and there was comfort in acknowledging it every day for a moment, and then returning to my life.

And the comfort wasn't just personal. As the weeks went on, we would see the new mourners with their fresh pain and loss, and know they, too, would eventually be four months, six months out, and find that they could breathe somewhat more easily again. And it was good to know our simple presence as fellow mourners could provide strength for someone new to grief.

So I stand here now enveloped by my tradition, embraced by a community and impressed by the wisdom of our faith. But what really surprised me at the end was when my sister's friend, who is not Jewish, lost her father. Suddenly, I wanted to suggest to her that perhaps saying the Kaddish might be a helpful way to start her life again. I knew it was ridiculous for her—I just felt it had been so right for us.

# Kaddish and How It Has Changed My Life
### By Michael S. Levin

KADDISH. Something I never dreamed of saying for my dad. I never dreamed of not saying it either. Frankly, even though my dad was eighty and living in Florida at the time, I had not spent a great deal of time contemplating the eventuality of what I would do when he passes away. He had not been sick. As a matter of fact, he was fairly vibrant for his age and got around quite well. He traveled to see his children and grandchildren until his unexpected and final illness. In fact, just two weeks before, he had the pleasure of seeing his grandson, my son, Jeff, graduate from Michigan State. This made him proud. My son's graduation ceremony was the last *simcha* in his life.

We sat Shiva at our house for the full seven days, as required by Jewish law. There was never any question that would be done. Coming from a Conservative upbringing, with observant Jews and even Rabbis in our family, I knew that we would have a full Shiva. It is what Dad would have wanted, what the family wanted and, even more importantly, what he deserved.

Saying Kaddish was something new to me. Regretfully, I did not say Kaddish for my mom thirteen years ago, possibly because of where I was in my life (small children, work, etc.), but I said Kaddish for Dad, for the full eleven months of mourning his death. I did not start out with a predetermined feeling that I was going to say it. In retrospect, after Shiva, my next "goal" was to say Kaddish for *Sheloshim*, the thirty-day period of mourning.

I began going to *minyan* at my synagogue every morning. At first, I felt alone and uncomfortable. I knew only one or two people who also were saying Kaddish at my synagogue, and the speed of the service and my lack of familiarity with it contributed to my feelings. I soon became more comfortable with the service; although even today, depending on who is davening, at times it is challenging to "keep up" with the service leader. I said Kaddish every morning during the eleven months and on a few evenings, too. My work precluded me from going twice a day, and I rationalized that once a day was enough.

During my week of Shiva, I "discovered" Friday evening services, our beautiful *Kaballat Shabbat*, welcoming the Shabbat, and rediscovered the blessings of Shabbat morning services.

I said Kaddish for the full eleven months. At first, it is fair to say, I did it for my dad. Toward the end, I was not only doing it for him but as much for myself, as well.

It is hard to describe the feeling of saying Kaddish for a parent. For me, it was something I, at first, felt obligated to do as a Jew and as a dutiful son. It turned out to be, in the short term, healing, comforting, and spiritually uplifting, so much so that I went from hoping that the eleven months and the commitment I had made would go quickly to not knowing what to do with myself upon completion of the required Kaddish period. The final time that I stood for Kaddish left me with an unexpected empty feeling. For eleven months, I had said Kaddish for my dad every morning. I had developed a routine and purpose in life which was now ending! What else could I do for him, now that Kaddish was completed?

In the long term, in my case, reciting Kaddish may have turned out to be a life-changing event.

It has now been almost one and a half years since my dad passed away. I am still going to morning *minyan* as frequently as possible, only now I go for myself and for others.

Although some mornings are awfully rushed, I still feel good putting on *t'fillin* and wrapping my *tallit* (prayer shawl) around my shoulders and back. I find the *minyan* to be a good way to start the day. I enjoy sharing a little of the morning with others who are going through or have gone through what I did. I continue to attend services on Shabbat. I have met many wonderful, warm, and caring people from my synagogue this past year and a half and no longer feel uncomfortable. I have also discovered the many Jewish Holidays that I never knew about, or had forgotten about, and the richness and demands of being a more observant Jew. I have learned a great deal and wish to continue learning and exploring this wonderful new life.

It is interesting that parents spend a lifetime teaching their children. Presumably, teaching ends when the parent dies. In my case, perhaps Dad's greatest lessons were learned from his death. He would be very happy to know that I have respected him through reciting Kaddish and that I have made Judaism an important part of my life again.

This was his final gift to me, and for this I thank him for eternity.

# My First Hebrew Words

## Joseph Piasecki

These reflections were inspired by an essay "Kaddish: An Opportunity to Comfort," by Herbert A. Yoskowitz, published in *The United Synagogue Review* (55/1), Fall 2002 (reprinted on page xv).

I lost my dad when I was six years old and an only child. His funeral was conducted from our home instead of a funeral home. It was quite an experience for a six-year-old. It left an everlasting impression. It was the first and possibly the only such funeral I can remember.

I was taught the "Kaddish Prayer" as my first experience with Hebrew. Whenever I recite or hear the Kaddish recited, it very vividly brings back the memory of that day, now seventy-two years ago. When you add to this the fact that my dad died just after the close of the Yom Kippur Service, you can understand the lasting impression that Kaddish made on my mind.

I wanted to explain that Kaddish is not just another prayer but a very thought-provoking piece of liturgy that is for me everlasting.

# Renewing, Reconnecting, Re-entering
## By Gail Raminick

My background and knowledge of Judaism has always been unimpressive and yet I have always felt very strongly about being Jewish and about the impact of our ancestors on the world. When my father died, I said Kaddish at home with my husband, Shel. I knew that would be fine with my father. And I knew that where I prayed would not be important to my father, or, in fact, if I prayed. My father knew how much Shel and I loved him.

After Shel's death, I went to the synagogue where we belonged, to say Kaddish in the evening. The service, mainly in English, was a very beautiful and moving one that was right for me at that time. My older son was attending services at Adat Shalom, and we both tried each other's places. That didn't work for us. He wasn't comfortable at my synagogue and I wasn't comfortable here. I stopped going to my synagogue after the first month. There were very few people at their evening service, and there was no morning service. Something that I needed just wasn't there!

At that time, Rabbi Yoskowitz said, "Gail, come to our services here, once or twice a week. Just give it a try and see if it helps you." So I came once or twice a week for a couple of weeks and then the once or twice a week became every day before work and I started to feel that I wanted to be here on Sunday, too. I don't know what draws me here, and I don't know what draws me to the cemetery on a weekly basis either. I just feel a magnetic pull, and I do what it leads me to do. For a reason that I don't really understand, I feel better being here. I don't read a word of Hebrew and can't always find where we are in the service. Some days I listen and read, and I see and hear only empty words. Some days those words are very meaningful to me. When I recite the words of the Kaddish, I think of my husband. I feel that this is something that I can do for him, for me and for us. Starting my day here gives me purpose. When I read the prayers and Psalms, I am looking for a spirituality that I need very much in my life. Shel had that spirituality. He never blamed God or anyone for his illness and always said, "It's the luck of the draw." He believed in God and he believed in us.

This has also become the place where I have re-entered the world without my husband. He will always be with me, but I have to learn to live as an "I" instead of a "we." Being in this accepting environment has been a good place to start. The friendships that I have made here are very important to me. Everyone cares about each other. We joke about our assigned seating, our attendance records, and sometimes we share a day that is harder than usual. We are all living with a hole in our lives and in our hearts. Some of our situations are easier to accept and rationalize than others, but we all have to manage. One of the women that I met here at Adat Shalom's morning service said, "Gail, when we started coming to say Kaddish, we were broken people. Now we are mending." Perhaps the words of the Kaddish do have a power to heal.

At the beginning I didn't know if I wanted to live without my husband. I just wanted to be with him. I still want to be with him somewhere, in some way, but the words from Psalm 30 on page 114 of the prayer book began to sink into my being. One line reads, "What profit is there in my death, when I go down to the grave? Shall the dust praise Thee? Shall it declare Thy truth?" I'm not sure what my truth is, but I know that I want to believe in God and in something that is beyond what is here. I also want to live the rest of my life in a way that will honor Shel and me.

45

# Saying Kaddish as the Anger Fades

By George Max Saiger

I was blessed to have both my parents alive until I was fifty years old. One thing that I came to believe with ever greater certainty as I got older was that I did not intend to say Kaddish for my parents every day for a year when it came time for them to die. I had long developed the habit of going to *shul* every Shabbat and Yom Tov. It was my expectation to say the Kaddish when, and only when, I was in *shul* anyway. Anything more seemed both onerous and meaningless, a deadly combination.

Then, one August evening, my mother died. Shiva was difficult for me. It was a mix of pain, tears, comfort, reflection, and boredom. We had a *minyan* in my house twice every day, as is the custom of my congregation. I was touched by the number of people who came to help make a *minyan*. At the end of it, the Rabbi stayed after the last morning service. "Put your shoes on," he said. "We are going for a walk around the block." I took off the bedroom slippers I had worn all week and went out for the first time. It was a nice summer day, perfect for a walk, perfect for getting back into my regular life. We talked about a variety of things, the Rabbi and I, including, I now remember, the idea that I should let the big Shiva candle burn itself out, letting Mother's soul linger in the house a bit longer. Then he left. At the door, he said, "*Minyan* at the *shul* this afternoon is at 6:05. See you then." Until that moment, I had not considered it—just as he had not considered that I wouldn't be there. I didn't see how I could respond to his warm support by starting a discussion about why I did not intend to go.

46

So I went. It was an odd experience. People greeted me with expressions of support, but I felt somewhat trapped by them and by the tradition. I remember feeling that they were welcoming me into the fellowship of the damned. And they were to be my *hevra* (fellow travelers) for a while. That first month, the time of sh'loshim, I felt mostly angry while I was in *shul*. I was angry that my mother was dead. I was angry that my prayers, and those of so many family and friends, for her recovery were not answered. I was angry that I suddenly had the burden of care of my ninety-two-year-old father. The icing on that bitter cake was my obligation to stand at the *ammud* (lectern), leading the congregation in prayers. Thus I was required to respond to my situation by intoning, over and over: "*Yitgadal v'yitkadash Sh'mei rabbah* . . . Magnified and sanctified is His great name." Inside I raged: "You can make me stand here. You can make me say these words. But You cannot make me accept that there is something right and holy about my mother being dead!"

I don't know when the anger began to fade. My last *hiyyuv* (obligation) as a mourner in sh'loshim was at *minchah* (the afternoon service), just before the beginning of Rosh HaShanah. I got there a few minutes late, and they held up that service, with hundreds of people there instead of the usual fifteen or twenty, waiting for me to lead them. "Hurry up, George, move it!" somebody said. I was touched—and maybe that's when I started to get less angry. Or maybe rage was just starting to wear thin already.

As autumn grew into winter, I found myself more welcoming of this new daily routine. I would often reflect about Mother during services, remembering this or that, and rather enjoying it. New mourners came, and now it was my turn to welcome them. Friendships grew out of that time. One, with Alan R., who started saying Kaddish about two months after I did, has continued ever since. We would negotiate which of us would lead which service and how long to wait for a *minyan*, or we'd just chat about nothing in particular while waiting.

In time this became routinized, just something I did every day. I decided again that I needed to make it become a conscious decision, so I purposely skipped a day here or there. It made me feel good, feel that I was still in control of my life. Consciously I had that mischievous good feeling on the mornings when I lay in bed an hour longer. Unconsciously it was even more important on those mornings when I did attend the *minyan*.

As spring came, it became clearer that this, too, would end. I couldn't bear to skip on purpose anymore, because there were so few days left in which I would have these minutes dedicated to my mother, *aleha hashalom* (may she be at peace). That addendum to her name had gradually crept into my feeling about her. It meant that Mother was now a memory, a soul which lingered ever more tentatively around the Kaddish, around the *minyan*, around my life.

And then it was over. I stood at the *ammud* for a while in silence after that last Kaddish.

"Hey, George," someone said, "the service is over. What's with you?"

"It was my last time," I answered.

There is an epilogue. Mother had died on *Rosh Hodesh Elul* [the first day of the Hebrew month of Elul]. I attended daily *minyan* for a while longer after my eleven months were over, no longer saying Kaddish. After the *yahrtzeit*, the special Psalm for *Elul*, "*L 'David HaShem Ori*" (Psalm XXVII) was added, to be recited twice daily during the month before and the month after Rosh HaShanah. One verse jumped out at me, one I hadn't noticed during *Elul* a year earlier, when I was just starting this journey. "For my father and my mother have left me, and God will gather me in." Daddy died a few years later, also in early *Elul*. This verse has become something of my ongoing Kaddish for them ever since.

48

# Watching My Father Say Kaddish

By David W. Schostak

My thoughts about the positive impact of the age-old tradition of reciting the Kaddish in memory of our loved ones are neither original nor out of the ordinary, but they are deeply personal.

I have two very vivid, yet very different experiences with saying Kaddish. The first occurred not as a direct result of my saying Kaddish, but had a permanent impact on my life. On May 5, 1970, seven months to the day before my Bar Mitzvah, my paternal grandfather passed away. My father had been raised in a Reform house, but with my mother, who chose to send us to Hillel Day School and who affiliated with the Conservative Movement, he chose to say Kaddish every morning and evening for the eleven months.

I don't know how it started, but my brothers and I began to go with my father every morning to Adat Shalom to say Kaddish with him. It became a morning ritual. He would wake us up, we would go to *shul* [synagogue] and then he would drop us off at Hillel Day School after services. Not only did it permanently enhance the bond among my brothers, our father, and me; it also contributed to our ability, even thirty years later, to lead the Shacharit service in the morning.

Even more interesting are permanent memories of that year and the links that were forged with the other members of the daily *minyan* who were also saying Kaddish. To this day, when I see those members, I fondly reflect back on the time that we spent together. When I occasionally read or hear of

49

their passing, it harkens me once again to the days when we used to go to *shul* with my father so he could say Kaddish for his father.

Unfortunately, twenty-six years later, almost to the day, my wife and I lost a child. And there again I found myself with the *need*, not just the obligation, to say Kaddish.

That experience was very much different from the one I had twenty-six years earlier with my father, because shortly after Shivah, we traveled to Israel for a previously planned trip for a joyous occasion, a *simcha*, the Bat Mitzvah of our niece. As a result, I spent all of *shloshim*, bouncing from one *shul* to the next, all over the State of Israel—sometimes in a Conservative setting, sometimes in an Orthodox setting, at other times in a Sephardic *shul*, but rarely in the same place twice.

Although I was clearly a stranger in each one of those synagogues, and literate in Hebrew, I was generally ignorant of their individual cultures and styles. Yet, I felt the immediate overwhelming warmth from all of the congregants, because they knew that I, too, was there to say Kaddish. I thought back to the time that I spent with my father when he was saying Kaddish. I remembered the bond that I had built with people who had become our very close friends as a result of that experience together. I realized that here I was with Jews from all over the world in Israel whom I did not know and never saw before and would never see again—but that same bond immediately existed when we said Kaddish together.

As a result of these two very different, yet similar experiences, I am convinced that it is God's infinite wisdom that mourners spend that time together. It not only helps their mourning and their healing, but builds lifelong relationships which enables everyone in mourning to gain something positive from their loss.

# The Brilliance of Our Tradition

Arlene F. Tilchin

I am halfway through saying Kaddish for my mother, who at ninety-four had a good and full life. I had said Kaddish for my father, who had died in 1991, when few women said Kaddish and women were not counted in the *minyan*. After Shiva for him, I knew that I could not get up and continue life as it was before. Our tradition had a place for me which was and is the daily *minyan*. I was there for the purpose of having set aside a special time twice daily for my father. This period gave me the opportunity to work through the heavy pain I and my family felt as my father's brilliant mind began to deteriorate and he became a person we didn't know, and who didn't know us.

As the months went on, these thoughts were replaced by those of the wonderful life that we shared. My father was in my thoughts all day, every day, and I kept smiling. My father was a deeply religious man. I felt that my father knew that I was saying Kaddish to honor his memory. My husband stood by me and said Kaddish for eleven months. For me, my husband's presence and voice validated the Kaddish for my father, by adding a male voice to the tradition that my father lived so fully.

I now attend *minyan* for my mother. As a counted participant saying Kaddish twice daily, I derive the same benefits that I did eleven years earlier. As I attend, I often think: what a wonderful role model she was. In the months that have followed her death, I have been able to draw on the example of

51

her life as a source of strength and inspiration. She was a devoted wife, mother, grandmother, and later a great-grand-mother and great-great-grandmother—a true woman of valor in so many ways.

In the early weeks after the death of my parents, when I came to the synagogue *minyan*, there was a community there who knew and understood my sadness. As I began to heal, I was there to be a source of healing to new mourners, as other mourners had been to me. The *minyan*, as a community, has the same personality as any group of people who have a common bond, and yet the *minyan* group is unique to itself. We start out as separate people, coming together because we all have suffered a loss, but soon integrate into a bonded community.

Now I realize the brilliance of our tradition when I under-stand that mourning is not an individual process. During Shiva, we are comforted by our community. Kaddish can be said only with a quorom and not independent of one. The mourning process reminds us again that for Jews "life is with people." In our tradition, it is appropriate to say to a mourner: "God shall comfort you in the midst of the rest of the other mourners in Zion and Jerusalem." It is this community of mourners that provides me with personal comfort and helps to perpetuate the memories that I want to hold dear.

# Linked to the Ancients

By Ellen Kurtzer White

*With loving thanks to the men in the back rows...*

It's time for me to leave my seat in the second row from the front on the right-hand side of the chapel at my reform congregation, Temple Beth-El, in Providence. I claimed this seat as mine nearly a year ago when my father died.

I was given one last chance to take care of my father. No more rides in ambulances. No more anxious pacing in emergency rooms. No more evenings at a nursing home trying to restore humor, light, and words to a man whose being had already left him. Instead my vigil was transformed into a routine and predictable task of sitting in a pew, standing at the end of the service and chanting Aramaic words that would hopefully secure safe passage for my father to the next world.

It never occurred to me that observing this tradition would create safe passage for me as well through this first year. For eleven months I had a space to grieve and to be supported. Every day, I heard my father's name read from the list of "the departed we now remember." I became linked to the woman in front of me, now widowed, and to the young man across the aisle with no mother. I became linked to the ancients who, in their wisdom, created a refuge for mourners, who understood the intense need to honor the dead and heal the living through time, community, and prayer. How immensely humane and holy in contrast to a contemporary culture that offers minimal and inadequate bereavement support. How immensely kind in the face of a secular world

53

whose pace has sped out of control and that has little tolerance for those who don't keep up even if mourning.

I can never say thank you enough to the "men in the back rows" whose commitment keeps the daily *minyan* alive. They are the keepers of a tradition grounded in wisdom and heart, and I have been blessed by their gift of being able to say Kaddish this year. The "Orchard Street Irregulars" with their Askhenazi accents, the jokes embedded with Yiddish and their memories of long-gone Jewish neighborhoods kept my father whispering in my ears this year. They are a blessing to this community and to the next person who takes a seat in the second row from the front on the right-hand side.

# Stronger Than Death

By Shoshana Wolok

My dear mother died in 1989. She was ninety-one years old, so there was not the anguish one feels when a child or sparkling young person dies. But a beloved mother is never old enough to die. I had loved and respected her all my life, and my heart was sore.

With this sore heart, I entered the daily chapel to begin a twice-a-day prayer regimen for eleven months. Rising to recite Kaddish gave me some way to express my love for my mother and to receive comfort. I soon saw this act as a way of bearing witness that **love is as strong as death** (Song of Songs 8:6).

It was soon apparent which individuals were coming to observe *yahrzeit* and which Kaddish. Praying together and sharing breakfast together day after day created a special bond. Each new Kaddish-observer was welcomed quietly and warmly. It finally seemed to me that the Kaddish group may well be the first and most durable support group in history.

But there were older men, retired men, who came morning after morning, who were observing neither Kaddish nor *yahrzeit*. They simply loved a program of daily prayer and felt needed (something often lost in retirement) to make sure that there was a *minyan*. I then remembered that, growing up, I had seen my father, *z"l* [abbreviation for Zichrono Livrachah, may his memory be for a blessing], every morning put on his *tallit* and *t'fillin* and recite the morning prayers. When he was home at late afternoon, he would go to the east wall, facing

Jerusalem, and recite the afternoon and evening prayers, *Minhah* and *Maariv* (he knew the prayers by heart). It was clear that being part of a "kingdom of priests" naturally involved a regimen of daily prayer.

Before Sukkot my husband and I flew to Israel for a six-week visit with our daughter, son-in-law, and three Israeli grandchildren. My Kaddish observance continued at the neighborhood Conservative Synagogue. In my heart, I said to my mother, "I am observing Kaddish for you in Yerushalayim. This is a great honor for you."

A few more months passed. The one thing that had seemed odd was that, in the hours of pain, we were reciting an ode of adoration to God. But one morning, as I was look-ing at the rising sun, the thought came to me, "How could God be so good to me as to give me such a wonderful mother, this wise and beautiful woman, this living personifi-cation of selfless love to her children, and a living example of the saintly person?" And then I understood that the recitation of Kaddish is an ode of Thanksgiving and totally appropriate.

Kaddish means that, when the Shiva and the condolence calls are over—when the house becomes silent, and the loss is sharp and intense—a Jew need not suffer alone. Comfort, fellowship, and emotional support are as close as the nearest synagogue.

# Remembering

By David Techner,
Ira Kaufman Funeral Home

In Melvindale, some skinhead kids had done some particular damage, and I was asked to go into the high school and address an assembly. At the time, I was president of the Michigan Funeral Directors Assembly, and happened to be the only Jew in the association.

During the question and answer session, a student came to the microphone and very respectfully asked this question: "Mr. Techner, I think you have a lot of guts to come here after this incident in this community and I appreciate your being here. But there is one thing I really would like to know. Why can't Jews forget the Holocaust?"

I was stunned by the question, although I didn't show it. It was a very thoughtful question based upon the discussion to that point. And I said to him, "Could you please repeat the question?" Now I must tell you that you could hear a pin drop when he asked the question. I replied: "Do you know anything about Judaism?" He said, "No, I don't." I asked if he ever had taken any comparative religion classes. And he said, "No, I have not." And I said, "Let me tell you a little bit about Judaism." And I proceeded to talk about Kaddish, about *Kibud Hamet* (the respect of the dead), about *Yizkor*, the synagogue services held four times during the year when the deceased family members and friends are remembered, about *Yahrzeit*, the Hebrew date of the death of family and friends on which we say prayers for the souls of our departed.

57

We go to services; we say Kaddish. On the four days during the course of the year, we have *Yizkor*. I looked at him and I said: "You see, it's not just the Holocaust; Jews don't forget about anybody."

Remembering our collective history and the histories of people whom we know is truly the hallmark of who we are as a people. To me, remembering our dead by saying Kaddish is one of the great beauties of being a Jew. Through the Kaddish Minyan, we become acquainted with other people who have suffered a similar loss. When we say the Kaddish together we are uplifted even as we give other Kaddish sayers our support.

# Avenues of Growth

By Rabbi Boruch E. Levin,
Hebrew Memorial Chapel

We know the importance of *mesorah* or "tradition" in our religion. It is interesting for me to see the deep conviction of people regarding this *mitzvah* of saying Kaddish. Jews who are otherwise detached from other areas of Jewish life have accepted upon themselves the responsibility of reciting the Kaddish for their departed loved ones. Although many of these mourners don't realize the rich heritage and importance of Kaddish, they still have this almost inborn feeling that urges them to recite the Kaddish in honor of the deceased. This feeling comes from an innate spark of *Yiddishkeit* that God has implanted in all of us. It reminds me of the Passover Seder in which most Jews participate, although their commitment to traditional Judaism might be minimal. It gives me personal strength when I realize how God put these rituals into our lives as guideposts and firm stepping stones in our journey through life.

I also find strength in the fact that God gives survivors not only a path of consolation through the observance of Shiva and in mourning rituals, but also an avenue of growth. We all know that there is a finality in death. A monument which describes the deceased's good deeds attests to that finality, by being etched in stone. Nothing changes, potential is nil and growth impossible—no additional *mitzvot*, no epitaphs changed. But the Kaddish sends its message—"*Yitgadal v'yitkadash shmay rabaw*—may God's great name be magnified and sanctified."

59

"By whom?" we should ask. "By us," must be the answer. Only if we, the survivors, reflect on the life that has passed, the parent that has taught, the link in our Jewish history that is now us, can we make some sense of what we are reciting. We are forced to ponder what legacy we received and maybe more importantly what legacy *we* will transmit. Personal growth, therefore, begs to be addressed head on— with the goal being "May God's great name be magnified and sanctified." God obviously does not need us to magnify and sanctify His name. Rather God has allowed us to do so to elevate our lives for our betterment, and for the betterment of all humanity. The Kaddish proclamation gives us direction—and therefore consolation. Death brought on unattachment. Kaddish brings on attachment—a deep feeling of belonging—to the past, present and future, to this golden chain that we call tradition or *mesorah* in our religion.

God in His infinite wisdom has given us Jews this precious practice of saying Kaddish, a practice which is so powerful and meaningful. The final ability to do one more concrete thing for Mom or Dad is most gratifying. It even gives the living a connection with the dead. Although death is final, it isn't as brutal. We don't feel as helpless.

# Comfort and Tranquility

By Jonathan M. Dorfman,
Dorfman Funeral Directors

As a practicing Jewish funeral director and psychologist for the past ten years, I have had the opportunity to assist families through one of the most difficult experiences in their lives. In dealing with these families and trying to comfort them and direct them on the path toward healing, I have found the Kaddish to be a very resourceful tool.

Judaism affords many unique and creative insights into death and mourning. It teaches that following the death of a loved one it is appropriate to say Kaddish for a period of eleven months, less one day, beginning from the date of death. The Kaddish gives the mourners guidance and hope in the face of great despair. I personally feel it teaches individuals to be strong, even when faced with a devastating loss. The prayer is traditionally said at the conclusion of the service after the lowering of the casket, which psychologically is one of the hardest aspects of the service. And during this emotionally draining period, the family and mourners and friends are standing side by side, shoulder to shoulder, and praising God's name. The beauty is not just in the words of the Kaddish but in the rhythm of the words. Saying it in the presence of others facilitates emotional healing (by outwardly expressing one's feelings and emotions). As a psychologist, I always say "grief shared is grief lessened," and it seems our ancient Tradition practices this insight. The Kaddish has helped our people from generation to generation and will continue to do so for generations to come.

In today's rapidly changing world, we need to seek comfort and tranquility in the stability of Tradition. Many people utilize Tradition only in times of great sorrow and duress. Fortunately, we have these customs to help guide us during these difficult periods in our lives. We must again thank and praise God for supporting us and for granting us life, thus embracing the precious words of the Kaddish.

# III.

## COMMENTING, LEADING AND MEDITATING ON THE KADDISH

### Linear Translation and Commentary on the Mourner's Kaddish

By Rabbi Daniel Nevins

#### INTRODUCTION
#### Genre

There are three major genres of Jewish prayer: praise (שבח), petition (בקשה), and thanksgiving (הודאה). The latter two genres relate to the needs and experiences of people, whereas the first focuses on the sanctity of God. Praise-prayers seek to transport the person beyond his or her own needs, and as such, are the purest liturgical form.

The rabbis classed several praise-prayers in a special category called "matters of sanctity" (דברים שבקדושה). These liturgical selections include the call to prayer (ברכו), the section of the reader's Amidah called "Kedushah" (קדושה), and the Kaddish (קדיש). All of these prayers require a *minyan*, a quorum of ten Jews who constitute a miniature version of Israel. While individual meditation is a praiseworthy and even necessary element of a spiritual life, Judaism instructs us that the Creator's praise is most impactful when announced in public. This requirement has sustained many a synagogue, as Jews learn to seek one another out in their goal of spiritual transcendence.

These "matters of sanctity" are all recited responsively, with a call and response interplay between a leader and the congregation. Their purpose is to sanctify God's name in this world, even as Isaiah described the angels' unceasing song in heaven.

## Language

The words of the Kaddish are an amalgam of Hebrew and scholarly Jewish Aramaic, which was the language of Jewish Torah scholars in the early Talmudic era. The familiar cadence of the Kaddish derives from the reflexive grammatical form (*Ithpael* in Aramaic; *Hitpael* in Hebrew) shared by ten of its opening words. Thus, *Yitgadal, v'Yitkaddash* in the first paragraph, and *Yitbarach, v'Yishtabach, vYitpoar, v'Yitromam, v'Yitnasei, v'Yithadar, v'Yitaleh, v'Yithalal* in the third paragraph, are all reflexive verbs that are nearly synonyms for God's exalted stature.

Aside from the pleasing cadence of this string of verbs, there is a theological message in their grammar. Rather than directly praising God, we ask that God be praised—it would be presumptuous to assume that we ourselves can cause God to be great. Moreover, this prayer praises not God's essence, but God's name. There is therefore deep humility and reverence embedded in the very grammar and diction of the Kaddish.

## Origins

The origins and original function of the Kaddish are shrouded in mystery. Its kernel is clearly the Aramaic verse from the book of Daniel (2:20), "May His great name be blessed forever and ever," which has a Hebrew equivalent in Psalms 113:2. This phrase, which is reverently referred to throughout Talmudic literature, became the cornerstone for the various versions of the Kaddish, which originated in

64

Palestine, and were developed further in Babylonia. The original use of the Kaddish had no connection to mourning; this association is first mentioned explicitly only in the thirteenth century. By that time, the legend of Rabbi Akiva saving a man's soul from perdition by teaching his son to recite Kaddish in synagogue had spread. This is apparently the ultimate cause for the medieval practice instituting קדיש יתום, the Mourner's (literally, orphan's) Kaddish. The Sephardic (and some Chasidic) traditions include in the first paragraph a request that God's redemption and messiah be delivered (ויצמח פרקנה וקרב משיחה).

Great and holy[1] shall His[2] great name[3] be in the world that He created by His will![4]

May His kingdom be established by your life and in your days[5] and in the life of the entire House of Israel.[6] Now, and speedily,[7] and say "Amen!"[8]

יִתְגַּדַּל וְיִתְקַדַּשׁ שְׁמֵהּ רַבָּא
בְּעָלְמָא דִּי בְרָא כִרְעוּתֵהּ
וְיַמְלִיךְ מַלְכוּתֵהּ
בְּחַיֵּיכוֹן וּבְיוֹמֵיכוֹן
וּבְחַיֵּי דְכָל בֵּית יִשְׂרָאֵל
בַּעֲגָלָא וּבִזְמַן קָרִיב
וְאִמְרוּ : אָמֵן

**May His great name be blessed[9] forever and ever![10]**

יְהֵא שְׁמֵהּ רַבָּא מְבָרַךְ
לְעָלַם וּלְעָלְמֵי עָלְמַיָּא

Blessed, acclaimed, glorified, elevated, raised high, beautified, exalted and praised[11] be the name of the Holy One, **blessed be He!**[12]

יִתְבָּרַךְ וְיִשְׁתַּבַּח
וְיִתְפָּאַר וְיִתְרוֹמַם וְיִתְנַשֵּׂא
וְיִתְהַדָּר וְיִתְעַלֶּה וְיִתְהַלָּל
שְׁמֵהּ דְּקוּדְשָׁא בְּרִיךְ הוּא

[God is] Beyond[13] all blessings, songs[14] praises and consolations that are said on earth, and say "Amen."

לְעֵלָּא מִן כָּל
בִּרְכָתָא וְשִׁירָתָא
תֻּשְׁבְּחָתָא וְנֶחֱמָתָא
דַּאֲמִירָן בְּעָלְמָא
וְאִמְרוּ : אָמֵן

May great peace come[15] from heaven and life for us and all Israel, and say "Amen."

יְהֵא שְׁלָמָא רַבָּא מִן שְׁמַיָּא
וְחַיִּים עָלֵינוּ וְעַל כָּל יִשְׂרָאֵל
וְאִמְרוּ : אָמֵן

May He Who makes peace above also make peace for us[16] and for all Israel, and say, "Amen."

עֹשֶׂה שָׁלוֹם בִּמְרוֹמָיו
הוּא יַעֲשֶׂה שָׁלוֹם
עָלֵינוּ וְעַל כָּל יִשְׂרָאֵל
וְאִמְרוּ : אָמֵן

—Mourner's Kaddish reprinted from
*Friday Night Alive!* © 1998 The Singlish Publication Society,
*www.singlishps.com.*

---

1. **Great and Holy**. Jewish theology balances two visions of God—transcendent and immanent. The transcendent vision of God—mighty, awesome, even frightening—is indicated by the first word, *Yitgadal* ("Great"). We often first think of God in terms of greatness, but Judaism seeks to move us to a more intimate relationship with God. The second word, *v'Yitkadash* (holy), is a source of connection between God and humans, for we are instructed to become holy via the commandments, even as God is known as The Holy One, Praised be He. This understanding of a God whom we can imitate is more immanent. Both modes of relating to God are necessary for a balanced Jewish perspective.

2. **His**. The masculine pronoun is here used to describe God, although the attributes of God alluded to in this prayer are alternately masculine and feminine in Jewish mystical theology.

3. **Great name**. We bless God's name but do not presume to comprehend or affect God's essence.

4. **In the world**. Isaiah envisioned the angels sanctifying God's name "in

the upper heavens." Our task is to make this created realm a laboratory producing holiness, thereby affirming the worth of our existence.

5. **By your life and in your days**. Is this phrase redundant, or does each word contribute new meaning? The former phrase implies that the totality of our lives should function to sanctify God, but that is a very tall order. In fact, Rabbi Akiva is said to have died satisfied (despite his tortured end) that he had fulfilled the command to love God "with all your being." For most humans, the method to accomplish this goal is much more mundane: through daily decisions to live a life of goodness. Thus "in your days" may be a more accessible way to sanctify God "by your life."

6. **The entire House of Israel**. Never underestimate the significance of our collective service to God. This prayer may not be uttered without a *minyan*, in fulfillment of the verse "I shall be sanctified in the midst of the children of Israel." (Leviticus, 22:32) God is said to rejoice in our unity, and to bemoan our division. When our collective existence becomes a *"Kiddush HaShem"* (sanctification of God's name), the redemption will surely be near.

7. **Now and speedily**. The messianic yearning of the Kaddish first emerges with these words. No mere recitation, this is an urgent demand addressed to the congregation to transform the world.

8. **Say "Amen!"** The congregation affirms all that the reader has said with this response, which is an acronym for the Hebrew words אל מלך נאמן (God, the faithful king). The Kaddish is essentially a call and response prayer.

9. **May His great name be blessed**. This is the kernel of the Kaddish, based on Daniel 2:20 and Psalms 113:2. The Talmud and commentaries (Shabbat 119b) emphasize that this response should be said vigorously, either through intense concentration or through raising one's voice in praise of God. Mystics read significance into the seven words and twenty-eight letters of this phrase, seeing it as a pillar of creation (seven days) and a source of strength (from the word כח "strength," whose numerical value is 28).

10. **Forever and ever!** An alternative understanding, based on the commentary *Metzudat David*, would be from this lower world to the supernal realm. In other words, may our humble praise resound across the heavens! The Jewish mystical tradition understands human actions on earth as impacting the heavenly realms beyond our comprehension.

11. **. . . and praised**. This concludes a string of eight verbs (in the reflexive grammatical form) praising God. Each word brings its own nuance but as a group they form a doxology, or powerful paean of praise. Added to the first two words of the Kaddish, we have ten verbs of

praise, corresponding to the ten mystical *sefirot* or dimensions of God's essence that are discernible to humans.

12. **Blessed be He!** This phrase is said by the reader and then repeated by the congregation. In some congregations, the response is "Amen."

13. **Beyond**. During the ten days of repentance from Rosh HaShannah through Yom Kippur, this phrase is replaced with לעלא לעלא מכל, "over and beyond all," because during this time we strive for an elevated spiritual sense even as God's sovereignty is more keenly apprehended.

14. **Blessings, songs**. In addition to being a prayer said by mourners, the Kaddish is used throughout the service to introduce or conclude various sections. This reference acknowledges that God is far greater than all of the praise that we utter in our liturgy.

15. **May great peace come**. Until this point, the Kaddish has offered pure praise of God. In a shift of genre, it now adds two Hebrew petitions asking for peace on earth.

16. **Also make peace for us**. This paragraph appears to repeat the message of the prior one, which also asked for peace. But while the former petition was oblique, asking "may peace come from heaven," the closing prayer is more insistent, asking that God intervene in the affairs of this world, sharing the heavenly peace with the people Israel during our lives. Nevertheless, the entire Kaddish prayer is extremely humble, never addressing God in the second person, and asking only for the most elevated of blessings, for peace.

# Leading the Kaddish: Impact on a Cantor

By Cantor Howard Glantz

As a young *chazzan* (cantor) just out of school, I remember feeling uncomfortable leading the Mourner's Kaddish at the daily *minyan* service with a quorum. After all, I was not a mourner, and I had vivid recollections of being urged to sit down in the chapel of my parents' *shul* as soon as the Mourner's Kaddish was announced in that only mourners stand for and say the Kaddish prayer in traditional circles.

The words were certainly familiar. Of all the liturgy in the *siddur* (prayer book) or *machzor* (prayer book for the High Holy Days), the Kaddish, in its various forms, is the most repeated text. The words rolled off my tongue as quickly as my telephone number and I enjoyed marking Shabbat and Holy Days with the traditional tunes and *nusach* (the traditional modes prescribed for chanting the liturgy). But somehow, leading people in a Mourner's Kaddish, I anticipated as being something very different.

Of course, I forged ahead performing this job requirement. Slowly and deliberately, I carefully enunciated each syllable of the Kaddish. As I became more and more accustomed to it, I viewed leading the Kaddish as a helpful task. With each person having a slightly different pace and pronunciation of this affirmation, I found that many could stay with the text easier having a leader to keep the pace steady and the words precise. Yes, it often struck me that I was not one of "them"—I had not experienced the obligation of saying the Mourner's Kaddish for a loved one; so I saw myself as

69

being unqualified for even the simplest of tasks associated with death. Even less so was I appropriate to be the one making the final prayers by the grave or comforting the mourners.

Logic didn't really play in these more-than-fleeting insecure thoughts. I knew rationally that I could be effective and helpful without having had an immediate loss. As I grew to know my congregation more intimately, I had occasion to witness deaths of several people with whom I had shared meaningful times. I experienced these losses personally; still, I was not obligated to Kaddish.

Then, almost three years ago, I received the news of my father's z"l death while enjoying a Caribbean cruise with my wife—the first vacation we had taken alone since the birth of our children. Being unable to leave the ship for three more days, the postponing of the funeral and the making of travel arrangements turned out to be no small feat. Suddenly I became aware of the wisdom in our heritage when I recalled the laws pertaining to the Onen (one whose immediate relative has died but whose funeral has not yet taken place). Despite this knowledge that I had no obligation to wear *tefillin* or to pray publicly, the feeling of being stranded drew me to the Friday evening service on the ship. When the Mourner's Kaddish was announced, I knew that I had to sit. Once I had seen to it that my father's z"l (of blessed memory) was resting properly could I be asked to affirm God's greatness in this awesome manner.

I remember practicing this moment in my mind and wondering if by some magic I was going to be "qualified" now. From that first Kaddish at the grave to the last Kaddish said at the *mincha* service eleven months from the date of burial, I had the strong feeling that I was being gradually strengthened through the experience and being assured that, in time, with God's help, it would be okay.

And today, while there are sad moments and memories in time, it is okay. I am once again not obligated to say the

Mourner's Kaddish daily. I thought that this discomfort of leading the congregation would be gone. However, it is more difficult, in that I can't help but remember what it was like for me during those eleven months.

# A Therapist's Response to Saying Kaddish

By Ruby E. Kushner, ACSW

As I write this, my father's passing is very recent, so the following is my conscious awareness as of now. The "now" is the amplified immediacy.

My mother's death five years ago propelled me into being my father's caretaker. Death transforms the living, and I grew in strength and patience and, I hope, kindness and generosity as I accepted the obligation.

I have been a psychotherapist for over twenty-five years, and worked with people of many faiths, from Catholics to Wiccans. I am no expert on comparative religions, but I am not aware of another faith, besides Judaism, that has so much reality and healing offered in its ritual as a way to cope with loss. Most religions have no healing ritual that extends beyond the funeral. The absence of form leaves people feeling confused, uneasy, adrift. They often have no experience with death and assume their reactions are abnormal. The eleven months of mourning for a Jewish parent, or the thirty days for a spouse, offer very realistic options, giving the mourner a way to adjust to the loss.

From a clinical point of view, there are two diagnostic categories: "brief depressive reaction" is an adjustment disorder with depressed mood; "prolonged depressive reactions" implies dysfunction. Judaism's prescription for mourning speaks to the first of these two, acknowledging the reality of time to adjust.

An antidote to depression is performing the required rituals. Thus, I have chosen to be at services at least once a day to say the Mourner's Kaddish. The observance and the physical effort of showing up at a specific time and place are concrete ways to counteract the sadness of my loss and to give my grief somewhere to go and something to do.

Other daily morning prayers, besides the Kaddish, evoke gratitude in me. They renew my appreciation for opening my eyes in the morning, for God's gifts to me of my parents, as well as for others who have blessed my life with their presence.

As I say the Kaddish, my mind uncovers more reasons to appreciate what my parents did for me. When I feel sad as I grieve for my parents' physical absence, the Kaddish lets me keep the sadness for now. In the future, I anticipate that the Kaddish will annually and seasonally allow for revisiting my losses.

The Kaddish offers me satisfaction as I recognize that I am saying Kaddish for my father just as he did for his. My joining in the Kaddish Minyan is a way to link me to my father and to his generation. Special to me are the familiar faces at the daily services, and the new faces who become part of the inner circle of those saying Kaddish, their nods, their greetings, their voices that join with mine when we say the Kaddish.

The support of the clergy is consoling as they invite me to share the story of my life. They, through their voices, words and dignity, give the Kaddish Minyan experience greater comfort and consolation for me.

Saying the Kaddish helps me to take care of my soul. The words and the rhythm of the Kaddish are a part of my healing as I give my grief somewhere to go and something to do in the process of mending my broken heart.

# Seven Dimensions of the Kaddish Minyan: A "Jewish Clinical" Look

By Rabbi Simkha Y. Weintraub, CSW

The Kaddish Minyan is one of the richest, soundest structures for the griefwork of bereaved individuals and families, a remarkable confluence of religious observance, spiritual impact, psychological insight, and emotional depth. It offers a range of resources, whose sum is more than simply the total of the parts. Consider these seven dimensions:

**A Place:** The loss of a close one pulls the rug out from under one's feet. A bereaved person may feel emotionally homeless, psychologically disoriented, and/or unwilling or unable to return easily to familiar contexts of life (home, work, social settings) that may once have been so comforting and effortless. The Kaddish Minyan, which often meets in a relatively intimate "daily chapel" of a synagogue, provides a place designated, among other central purposes, for the mourner. The world at large may urge one to "move on," to somehow return to one's former self, to an earlier and easier script—but in the place of the Kaddish Minyan it is critical to be touched by the past, and one is expected not only to remember but to reaffirm one's shifting but ongoing connection to the departed.

Recall how, in greeting the mourner in the days following the loss, Jewish practice suggests the blessing "May the *Makom* (literally "the Place," one traditional way of referring to God) comfort you among all the mourners of Zion and Jerusalem." The Kaddish Minyan offers a sense of that Place.

**People:** After a loss, one natural reaction is to withdraw, to pull inwards, to buffer oneself against stimuli (including, but not only, painful or challenging stimuli) in one's vulnerable and exposed state. Over time, one gradually begins to let others in and to reach out to others, and the Kaddish Minyan offers the perfect cohort and context for this incremental reopening. Some participate in the *minyan* simply out of a basic, general commitment to communal Jewish prayer, unrelated to loss, but others may be there to commemorate the annual *yahrzeit* of a beloved one, or to help ensure the quorum of ten, and some with a recent, gaping personal wound. Each requires the other for the community to somehow join in praising God, despite the profound hurts they have sustained and irreparable absences they endure.

**Perspectives, Purposes:** As time moves on, the stories of the other mourners and community members in the Kaddish Minyan can become a unique source of insight and reflection. Their experiences and insights may support and even inspire, and they may offer some very practical guidance (*Where can I donate his clothes? How can I attend an upcoming family wedding? How did you decide on the tombstone's wording? Etc.*). Reflected in the faces and words of others, one's own journey is enhanced and deepened, and certainly rendered more bearable and intelligible. The fellow travelers of the Kaddish Minyan may constitute an invaluable family for both grief and renewal, representing a chorus of related voices, a treasury of helpful ideas.

**A Pastor:** Very often, the rabbi, cantor, or *shammes* (sexton), or lay leaders committed to the *minyan*, become valuable pastoral and spiritual supports. They may serve as special listening ears or dependable shoulders; they may help with questions of ritual practice or theological issues. They may teach or guide, respond or model. On Monday and Thursday mornings, when the Torah is read, or on *Rosh Hodesh*/The New Moon, or around Jewish holidays, they may share helpful and inspiring *Divrei Torah*/Words of Torah. For many, drawing closer to the clergy "up there on the *bimah*" is part of a de-mystification of Jewish religious tradition and Jewish spiritual life, that opens doors previously shut.

**Prayer:** Loss and suffering have a muting effect on people. The Kaddish, is, of course, central to the *minyan*, and over the weeks and months, it becomes a shared mantra-like chant to help carry one forward in one's grief and mourning. But other prayers, psalms, and readings may also expand in their meaning and relevance, and open up as containers for deeply felt emotions, profound values, and fundamental beliefs. Certain tunes may emerge as particularly comforting; certain lines (for example, from psalms) may serve to express one's current state of spirit—hopeful, lonely, grateful, despairing, searching, etc. The experience of prayer—both communal and personal, fixed and spontaneous—may unfold as more accessible and more involving than before. At one and the same time, a mourner may develop a traditional repertoire *and* a highly individual voice of prayer.

**A Plan, a Path:** Loss leads so often to depression, which, in turn, is often manifest in a frozen state of inaction, a tendency to want to "stay under the blankets" and do little. To an extent, that inclination, that *need*, must be respected and indulged, but it can easily become maladaptive, compounding depression and misery. The commitment to challenge one's crippling sadness by joining a Kaddish Minyan may constitute a first step of re-empowering oneself, of embarking on a path, following a plan of re-entry. So much can seem uncertain, so many routines may appear meaningless—but the regular participation in a Kaddish Minyan counteracts purposelessness and gives one something to do, precisely when it feels that there is nothing one *can* do.

**Presence and Peace:** In the course of time, the Kaddish ritual enables one to integrate painful losses into one's life story—never to forget, but rather to increasingly draw on memory for its healing potential. What once may have triggered only great pain and emptiness now fosters a measure of solace and wholeness. Memory, at first a pointer to what is no longer, now feeds a sustaining vision of what was, and what can be. Like the very experience in a Kaddish Minyan, we realize that we are part of an eternal people, that all must cope with pain and loss, and all can reach, together, for hope and transcendence. We sense, we affirm, we pray: *God will bring peace, not only to me/us, but to All: Amen.*

---

Readers may be interested in an essay by Dr. Saul Scheidlinger, "The Minyan as a Psychological Support System," which appeared in the August 1997 *Psychoanalytic Review* (84, 4).—SYW

# Meditations

## The Tradition of the Kaddish

The origins of the Kaddish are mysterious; angels are said to have brought it down from heaven. . . .

It possesses wonderful power. Truly, if there is any bond strong enough to chain heaven to earth, it is this prayer. It keeps the living together, and forms a bridge to the mysterious realm of the dead. One might almost say that this prayer is the . . . guardian of the people by whom alone it is uttered; therein lies the warrant of its continuance. Can a people disappear and be annihilated so long as a child remembers its parents?

Because this prayer does not acknowledge death, because it permits the blossom, which has fallen from the tree of humankind, to flower and develop again in the human heart, therefore it possesses sanctifying power.

(Excerpted from the *Gates of Prayer*, copyrighted by the Central Conference of American Rabbis and reprinted by permission.)

## The Kaddish

The Kaddish is not a prayer for the dead, but a mandate to the living. It bids us rise above our sorrow, and fixes our view upon the welfare of humanity. It lifts our hope and directs our vision to a day when all shall at last inhabit the earth as children of the one God, when justice shall reign supreme, in peace.

—Richard C. Hertz

(Quote is from *Siddur Hadash for All Sabbath & Festival Services*, edited by Rabbis Sidney Greenberg and Jonathan D. Levine, page 47. Copyright 2000 by The Prayer Book Press of Media Judaica, Inc., Bridgeport, CT 06605. Reprinted by permission.)

"The loving kindness which we show to the departed is the ultimate form of loving kindness" (Rashi).

One of the most tender examples of such loving kindness is the recitation of the Mourner's Kaddish during the Period of Mourning and on the anniversary of a loved one's death. As we remember our departed, we perpetuate their presence among us. By remembering them we confer upon them the gift of immortality.

—Sidney Greenberg and Jonathan D. Levine

(Quote is from *Siddur Hadash for All Sabbath & Festival Services*, edited by Rabbis Sidney Greenberg and Jonathan D. Levine, page 47. Copyright 2000 by The Prayer Book Press of Media Judaica, Inc., Bridgeport, CT 06605. Reprinted by permission.)

## A Personal Meditation

Eternal God, Master of mercy, give me the gift of remembering. May my memories of the dead be tender and true, neither diminished by time nor falsified by sentimentality. Let me recall them, and love them, as they were. Grant me the gift of tears. Let me express my sense of loss, my sorrow, my pain, as well as my gratitude and my love. Bless me with the gift of prayer. May I confront You with an open heart, with trusting faith, unembarrassed and unashamed. Strengthen me with the gift of hope. May I never lose faith in the beauty of life, the power of goodness, the right to joy. May I surrender my being, and the soul of the dead, to Your eternal compassion.

(Reprinted from *Siddur Sim Shalom*,<br>edited by Rabbi Jules Harlow, page 518.<br>Copyright by The Rabbinical Assembly, 1985.<br>Reprinted by permission of The Rabbinical Assembly.)

# A Yizkor Meditation in Memory of a Parent Who Was Hurtful

By Bob Saks

Dear God,
You know my heart.
Indeed,
You know me better than I know myself,
so I turn to You
before I rise for Kaddish.

My emotions swirl as I say this prayer.
The parent I remember was not kind to me.
His/Her death left me
with a legacy of unhealed wounds,
of anger
and of dismay
that a parent could hurt a child as I was hurt.
I do not want to pretend to love,
or to grieve what I do not feel,
but I do want to do what is right
as a Jew and as a child.

Help me, O God,
to subdue my bitter emotions
that do me no good,
and to find that place in myself
where happier memories may lie hidden,
and where grief for all that could have been,

all that should have been,
may be calmed by forgiveness,
or at least be soothed by the passage of time.

I pray that You,
who raises up slaves to freedom,
will liberate me from the oppression
of my hurt and anger,
and that You will lead me from this desert
to Your holy place,
Amen.

# Selective Bibliography

Brener, Anne. *Mourning and Mitzvah*. Woodstock: Jewish Lights, 1993.
———. *Taking The Time You Need to Mourn Your Loss*. (Life Lights). Woodstock: Jewish Lights, 2000.
De Sola Pool, David. *The Kaddish*. New York: Sivan Press, 1964.
Diamant, Anita. *Saying Kaddish*. New York: Schocken, 1998.
Gillman, Neil. *The Death of Death, Resurrection and Immortality in Jewish Thought*. Woodstock: Jewish Lights, 1997.
Goldberg, Chaim. *Mourning in Halahah*. New York: Mesorah, 1999.
Greenberg, Sidney (Editor). *A Treasury of Comfort*. Hollywood: Wilshire, 1967.
Hoffman, Lawrence A. *Canonization of the Synagogue Service*. London: University of Notre Dame Press, 1979.
Klein, Issac. *A Guide to Jewish Religious Practice*. New York: The Jewish Theological Seminary of America, 1992.
Kolatch, Alfred J. *The Jewish Mourners' Book of Why*. New York: Jonathan David, 1993.
Lamm, Maurice. *The Jewish Way in Death and Mourning*. New York: Jonathan David, 1994.
Levine, Aaron. *To Comfort the Bereaved: A Guide for Mourners and Those Who Visit Them*. New Jersey: Jason Aaronson, 1996.
Riemer, Jack (Editor). *Jewish Reflections on Death*. New York: Schocken, 1974.
Scherman, Nosson. *The Kaddish Prayer*. New York: Mesorah, 1997.
Solomon, Lewis D. *The Jewish Book of Living and Dying*. New Jersey: Jason Aaronson, 1999.
Spitz, Elie Kaplan. *Does the Soul Survive? A Jewish Journey to Belief in Afterlife, Past Lives and Living With Purpose*. Woodstock: Jewish Lights, 2000.
Steinsaltz, Adin. *Simple Words*. New York: Simon & Schuster, 1999.
Telsner, David. *The Kaddish: Its History and Significance*. Jerusalem: Tal Orot Institute, 1995.
Wieseltier, Leon. *Kaddish*. New York: Knopf, 1998.
Wolfson, Ron. *A Time to Mourn: A Time to Comfort*. New York: The Federation of Jewish Men's Clubs, 1993.

# Index

**Herbert A. Yoskowitz** is a Rabbi of the Adat Shalom Synagogue, Farmington Hills, Michigan. He holds a master of arts degree in clinical psychology from the University of Florida, as well as a master of Hebrew literature degree, Rabbinic ordination and honorary doctor of divinity degree from The Jewish Theological Seminary of America. The author of numerous articles and book reviews, Rabbi Yoskowitz has served on the editorial board of *Conservative Judaism* magazine. He has received specialized training in crisis and chemical dependency counseling, with special emphasis on bioethics, and has served in local, regional and national leadership positions with the Conservative Jewish Movement.

www.ingramcontent.com/pod-product-compliance
Lightning Source LLC
Chambersburg PA
CBHW071353090426
42738CB00012B/3104